Dear Friends,

Patriots Day in the Commonwealth of Massachusetts is a civic holiday which commemorates the Battle of Lexington and Concord, the beginning of the American Revolution, and the spirit of independence and personal determination that gave rise to it. Since 1897, Patriots Day has been celebrated annually with the running of the Boston Marathon, the world's oldest continually contested marathon. Over 117 years, the Boston Marathon has been witness to the rise of legends in our sport, the exponential growth of the running community, and unforgettable stories of personal triumph.

Each Patriots Day, the strength and resilience of the worldwide running community is on full display as thousands of runners accept the challenge of the 26.2-mile run from Hopkinton to Boston. At the core of this event is the determination that propels each participant through eight cities and towns along the historic course. From many of the world's best marathoners on a quest for the champion's laurel wreath, to runners chasing a personal best or raising funds for local charities, to nearly 500,000 spectators who line the course, the Boston Marathon is an iconic spectacle in the world of sport.

We at the Boston Athletic Association are priveleged to carry on the tradition of this event, which is so special to the City of Boston, the town of Hopkinton, all of the cities and towns along the route, all of the people of Greater Boston, and our sport as a whole. On Patriots Day, we are all one community. We salute all who are passionate about the Boston Marathon and the sport of running, and we hope that your dedication and strength will bring all of you here to run with us.

Sincerely,

Thomas S. Grilk
B.A.A. Executive Director

THE BOSTON MARATHON
A CELEBRATION OF AMERICA'S GREATEST RACE

TOM DERDERIAN

TRIUMPH
BOOKS

TRIUMPHBOOKS.COM

This book is available in quantity at special discounts for your group or organization.
For further information contact:

Triumph Books LLC
814 N. Franklin
Chicago, Illinois 60610
www.triumphbooks.com

PRODUCTION
Susan Van Etten, Photo Research
Eileen Wagner, Design
Ashley Van Etten, Illustration

Printed in USA

ISBN 978-1-60078-939-7

CONTENTS

Foreword
by Bill Rodgers

Having been asked to write the Foreword for this new edition of the Centennial Boston Marathon book, I felt equal parts tradition or fear and excitement or honor at the thought of writing about my favorite race. I felt the anxiety one feels before a race. This is because I am no writer! Yet I feel a lot for this marathon, as much as anyone who has challenged himself (or herself) by running it does.

Tom Derderian, the author of this book and my friend, teammate, and training partner in the Greater Boston Track Club in the seventies, feels a lot for this marathon too. He has run the marathon, sub 2:20

Bill Rodgers.

for 18th place in 1975 (the year I first won), and has researched and written about the Boston Marathon's history in several award-winning books. His love for this race shows in these skillfully written very short stories of the race.

I love the history of the marathoners' excellence, which the Boston Marathon personifies. I learned a sense of this history under the tutelage of 1968 Boston champion Ambrose Burfoot, who was a college cross-country and track teammate at Wesleyan College in Middletown, Connecticut, when he won. Ambrose had his own Boston marathon mentor in the person of John J. Kelly, who won in 1957. Mr. Kelly was Ambrose's high school English teacher and cross-country coach. My point is that this Marathon has a special place in New England hearts—and in the hearts of all committed marathoners both in the U.S. and around the world. One hundred and seventeen years of consecutive races will do that for you. There is no other marathon with such a history of the world's top marathoners racing over the same course. Thus Boston stands alone in that regard and, with its qualifying standards, it has become the equivalent of the Olympic marathon for the most committed of our runners.

This gem of a race has not made it to this point without growing pains. Some of these were quite well known: the Kathy Switzer/Jock Semple clash in 1967, the Rosie Ruiz charade in 1980, the rope-start tripping debacle of 1987, and the wheelchair crashes of 1987. These "flaws" in the race got worldwide attention because the race in Boston has always been at the forefront of the sport as it evolved.

In fact the race went from a 17th century trot to a 21st century professional athlete's event in one year: 1986. That was the year that the race organizer, the Boston Athletic Association, agreed to the introduction of prize money, generously supplied by current title race sponsor John Hancock Financial Services. The Boston Marathon has become a far stronger and better-managed event ever

since. Twenty-three thousand runners were at the starting line at Hopkinton in 2013, and almost all qualified by running other marathons in the same year under a specific time limit determined by one's age.

The runners who don't time qualify get their numbers in a unique and admirable manner: they raise money for one of 15 special race beneficiaries, such as the Jimmy Fund, Team Diabetes, or Special Olympics. These runners are making a strong effort of the most positive kind in our country. They're giving of themselves to help conquer diseases that may strike many of us. This program got its start under longtime race director Will Cloney, who worked with the MS Society beginning in 1975 to raise dollars in this method.

All of this is good. But would it exist today if Johnny Kelly hadn't had his heart broken when he lost the race on that big hill at the 21-mile mark near Boston College; if mighty Clarence DeMar hadn't won seven Bostons in his immutable manner in the twenties and thirties? Talk about the American individual standing alone and conquering all! He was the real Marathon Man, unafraid of all challenges, prepared to do his best facing the adversity that 26 miles of road presented.

And what of the great women at Boston! What of the then–world record race of Joan Benoit Samuelson of Maine in 1983? Would that have happened if Roberta Gibb hadn't become the first woman to run the Boston Marathon in 1965? What about the real champion of the 1980 Boston Marathon, the year Rosie Ruiz attempted to steal the race? If that was a low point, surely Jacqueline Gareau's gracious sportsmanship is a high point for all marathoners. Kenya's Margaret Okayo set a new course record in 2002. Catherine Ndereba of Kenya conquered the course four times. Could they have done this without Sara Mae Berman's (unofficial) win two decades earlier, when the women champions weren't given the gold medal emblazoned with the Unicorn, symbol of the race and of the B.A.A.? Would there be an absolute take-over of the city's finest hotels and restaurants, as there is today on race day, if we hadn't been given a bowl of beef stew after the finish in the sixties and seventies? Would those fine, lithe Kenyans be running Boston today if 176-pound Joe "Milkman" Smith hadn't thrashed himself to win more than 70 years ago? Would

there be a wheelchair competitors' world championship at Boston today if Bobby Hall hadn't pushed to victory alone in a standard wheelchair—a true pioneer—in 1975?

Today there are few pretenders to the throne that Boston occupies. That's all they can be. History cannot be denied on this scale. Long live the Boston Marathon! Now you know how I feel about this race. But I'm not alone. Come to Boston on Patriots Day and watch and listen as a million Massachusetts citizens show their feelings for the runners in this special race. The Boston Marathon produces what I feel is the best in American sports. Both small town America and big city America come together in this race as in no other.

Introduction

I wrote this book from a different point of view than most books about the Boston Marathon—the perspective of the spectators and the residents along the much-storied road from Hopkinton to Boston. *The Boston Marathon: A Celebration of America's Greatest Race* shows that while the marathon is in each town, it belongs to that town—remember, only about three of the twenty-six miles are in Boston proper.

In keeping with this motif, you'll find within these pages moments, like snapshots, from the history of the race and its people, both runners and watchers—for the Boston Marathon belongs as much to those who watch as to those who run. Without the cheers of the people along the way, the blood and sweat of the racers would be for nothing.

I wrote *The Boston Marathon: A Celebration of America's Greatest Race* to celebrate those who watch the Boston Marathon and those gracious residents who welcome a population of runners that at times exceeds the populations of the very towns they pass through. I have added five new essays. The true "owners" of the Boston Marathon are not the Boston Athletic Association or the sponsors. This book is for the real hosts—those along the roadside.

HOPKINTON

ASHLAND

FRAMINGHAM
TRAIN DEPOT

ASHLAND
CLOCK TOWER

90

5K

W Union St

Union St

Chestnut St

HOPKINTON STATE PARK
P (Parking with
shuttle to start)

START LINE
1897-1923

START

EXIT
21A/21B

St

135

E Main St

STYLIANOS
KYRIAKIDES
STATUE

Highland St

Pond St

126

REET LOT
g with
e to start)

Grove St

HOPKINTON

85

Boston Marathon®

jetBlue

FINISH

FRAMINGHAM

NATICK

HALF

WELLESLEY

NEWTON

BROOKLINE

BOSTON

START

HOPKINTON

BOSTON MARATHON®
Official JetBlue Course Map

Gatorade and Poland Spring
are available to runners at
every mile mark along the
course and at the finish line

Hopkinton

The town of Hopkinton is where the Charles River and the Boston Marathon start, both of them ending in Boston proper. Incorporated as a town on December 13, 1715, Hopkinton started as a farming community. Then in the 1800s it became a shoe manufacturing center. Now it is a growing, prestigious suburb of Boston with more than 13,000 residents.

Hopkinton still harbors some of its agricultural past in acres of nursery land for growing trees and shrubbery on the grounds of the Weston Nurseries located at the one-mile mark of the Marathon.

The town sits at an altitude of 490 feet above sea level. The Marathon's starting point was moved here from Ashland in 1924.

Movable Go

Today, the site of Metcalf's Mill in Ashland, where the first Boston Marathon started in 1897, is an overgrown hole in the ground. There is not even a plaque, since the site was abandoned by the B.A.A. in 1900. The mill, which manufactured shoe boxes, burned in the thirties, and nothing has been built in its place.

Dick Fanon of the Ashland Historical Society at the site of Metcalf's Mill.

The next starting point for the race was in the middle of a railroad bridge. Then in 1907 the start moved to Steven's Corner and again in 1924 to Hopkinton. It was here that the course was lengthened to 26 miles, 385 yards, to match the international marathon standard. But the start hopped around Hopkinton a few more times. It moved west in 1927, and west again in 1957. Then it moved around the corner to Hayden Row in 1965, and back east in 1986 to where it is today.

The start of a Boston Marathon that Clarence DeMar won.

Ronald MacDonald The First Winner from Massachusetts?

Ronald J. MacDonald won the Boston Marathon in 1898 while a student at Boston College and affiliated with the Cambridgeport Gymnasium in Massachusetts. But MacDonald always considered himself a Canadian, and he later returned to his native Antigonish, in Nova Scotia, and became a medical doctor. He practiced medicine in Newfoundland for 30 years. He eventually returned to Antigonish and died there on September 3, 1947.

A *Boston Herald* illustration from 1898 of Ronald MacDonald.

The Start Is Not Fair

The start of the Boston Marathon on what was once a country road cannot be fair to all the runners. The road is so narrow that fewer than 50 runners can line up in the front row. Only the top 100 seeded runners can expect to start running the moment the gun is fired. The 5,000th runner across the starting line is officially allowed to subtract more than five minutes from his finishing time to correct for the start.

 With up to 20,000 official runners, it may take the last runners half an hour or more to reach the starting line. By then, the leaders will be five miles away. It would be ideal if all runners could get a fair start, but nowhere in Massachusetts could 20,000 runners line up shoulder to shoulder.

Shoulder to shoulder at the 1988 start.

Did you know?

The Lottery for Starting Numbers

To maintain control over the number of official entrants to the 1996 Boston Marathon and to reduce the number of "bandits" (unofficial runners), the B.A.A. instituted a lottery system. All runners who had earned qualifying times in their age groups could automatically enter. Other entrants were included by lottery until the size of the field reached the limit established.

The First International Field

The first Boston Marathon runners from outside the U.S. were Canadians who came to race in 1900, accompanied by an entourage of "businessmen" who intended to profit. The Boston Marathon was the lottery of its day, and the backers planned to snooker well-heeled Bostonians with exorbitant bets. Most of the serious spectators took the train to the start, and the betting took place on board. Bostonians thought they knew marathons and so accepted apparently foolish foreign wagers, some on a sweep, others on win, place, or show.

So tense were the runners that this race produced the first and only false start in Boston Marathon history. Once the runners had taken off on the second start, the Canadians dominated the race and swept the top three positions. Their backers cleaned up.

The First Woman

There were no women in the first 69 Boston Marathons. It took a woman of unconventional wisdom to attempt to run a whole Boston Marathon. It was feared that running long distances would be damaging to women. These were men's fears, not women's, but men were in charge of the race. So the woman who ran for the first time, in 1966, snuck into the race, running unofficially and without a number.

Roberta Louise Gibb was (and still is) unconventionally wise. She did not approach the Marathon headlong, as did most men. The men had run track in high school and college and then graduated to longer distances, culminating in the Marathon. Roberta Gibb started with the Marathon, although she approached it obliquely, as an artist. She saw the race not as a contest, but as a thing of beauty. She wanted to be part of the pageant, not to beat anyone, not to prove anything, but to join the flow of runners moving through the towns of greater Boston. And her approach yielded the thoroughly athletic time of 3:21.

Roberta Gibb at work in her studio.

Massive Collision

Wheelchair racers like to go fast. That is the whole point of racing. Downhill the chairs can reach speeds of 30–40 mph, and the start of the Boston Marathon shoots sharply downhill. In the 1987 race, the wheelchairs started aggressively. These were tough and seasoned athletes, each of whom wanted to win. But an unreproduceable chain of events led to wheelchairs suddenly flying in all directions. Some tangled, some tipped, some slid.

To the racers in the chairs, it was just part of racing. But the public was horrified. The wheelchair racers hate it when people feel sorry for them. They want to be regarded as the athletes they are, athletes who train hard and race furiously. They are willing to take the same kinds of risks bicyclists and other athletes take. However, public sensibilities also have to be addressed, so a controlled start was instituted to prevent crashes.

A wheelchair collision in 1985.

How Marathon Racing Began

There were no marathon races in the world before 1896. The ancient Greeks did not have a marathon in the original Olympics. Their longest footrace was about five kilometers. It was held in a stadium and run on loose sand back and forth around two posts. Kicking, shoving, fighting, and sand throwing were allowed—not the kind of race we have inherited today.

A black-figured amphora showing three racers at the Panathenaic Games.

French nobleman Pierre Baron de Coubertin is often credited with inventing the modern marathon in 1894. Coubertin initiated a revival of the ancient Olympic Games. His friend Michel Breal, a professor at the Sorbonne, persuaded him to include a long footrace, and the organizers of the first modern Olympic Games, held in Athens, planned one to commemorate the Battle of Marathon in 490 B.C. Breal offered a silver cup to the winner of that first marathon.

At the End of Their Rope

The necessity of sticking to tradition led to a near disaster at the start of the 1987 Boston Marathon. That year, officials held a rope over the starting line and ushered runners behind it. The purpose of the rope was to prevent false starts. Unfortunately, the official starter did not communicate with the officials at either end of the line and was unaware that their watches were not in sync. The starter looked at his watch and, while the rope was still waist-high, raised his pistol and fired it.

The field charged. The 5,315 runners did not know that the rope remained tight. It trapped Australian Rob de Castella, who rolled to the ground but bounced back up, now in 50th place, but still game to chase the leaders. De Castella had set a course record the year before, and he again worked his way up to the front pack. But he was racing tired and could not overtake them. He finished sixth and did not blame the rope or the tumble for his loss.

The start at Hopkinton in 1987.

Hopkinton "Common" Hospitality

Jeff and Sue Hadley live on Hopkinton Common and open their house to marathon runners every year. The same runners come back to use the bathroom or borrow a smear of Vaseline, a bandage, or a glass of water. Some leave their clothes and return to hobble up the stairs late in the afternoon to retrieve them. The party starts early at the Hadleys'. Since the roads close at 8:30 A.M., they begin the festivities an hour earlier with breakfast.

The Arlington Trotters are guests of the Hadleys.

Just up Hayden Row at the Wilsons', the entire state of Oklahoma seems to be strewn about the house. The Wilsons have lived in the colonnaded house for 30 years and open their doors yearly. They have adopted the runners from Oklahoma City, and they hang the Oklahoma flag outside their house to welcome their regulars.

Across the street is the George Buckholtz "Texas" house with the welcome mat out for runners from Texas. Many houses in Hopkinton give hospitality to specific running clubs from all over the country. And the Hopkinton residents' extraordinary hospitality is accepted with thanks, letters, photographs, even engraved plaques of gratitude from their guests.

The Brown Family

Who gets to fire the starting gun for the Boston Marathon? As with nearly everything in the Boston Marathon, tradition dictates.

In 1905, George V. Brown started the race. An employee of the B.A.A. at the time, he became athletic director for Boston University and then general manager of the Boston Arena, where the B.A.A. indoor track meet was held. Later, when wealthy B.A.A. member Henry G. Lapham gained control of Boston Garden, Brown became general manager and a member of the B.A.A.

George V. Brown served as Marathon starter until he died in 1937. His son Walter A. Brown succeeded him both as general manager of Boston Garden and as starter of the Marathon. It was Walter who organized the Boston Celtics basketball team and the Boston Bruins hockey team. He became president of the B.A.A. in 1940 and served until his death in 1964.

Tom Brown served as starter for the next several years. Since 1991, Walter A. Brown's nephew, Walter F. Brown, has started the race.

Tom Brown starting the race in 1986.

Setting Women's World Records

In the first few years of the women's Boston Marathon, every official winner set a course record. Then in 1975, Liane Winter, a 33-year-old accountant for Volkswagen from Wolfsburg, West Germany, bested her personal record by eight minutes to break the Boston Marathon course record and set a women's world record in the process.

Liane Winter.

The next woman to break the women's world record at the Boston Marathon was Joan Benoit. The first time she won the Boston Marathon was in 1979. In the next three years, she trained and over-trained, adhering strictly to a training schedule of ever-increasing mileage. She missed two Boston Marathons and placed a disappointing third in 1981. But she knew deep inside that she could run a marathon faster than any woman had ever run.

Joan Benoit.

In 1983, Allison Roe held the women's world record, and she knew that Grete Waitz planned to break it in London the day before the Boston Marathon. So Roe phoned Benoit and asked her if she would like to run together, but Benoit declined.

Benoit blasted off at the start with a reckless pace. She reached the halfway point at a pace that would have broken the world record by nearly 10 minutes. She slowed a great deal over the last miles of the course but still broke the world record by nearly three minutes.

The West House

Marge West and her husband, George, live on the private property closest to the Marathon's starting line. They cherish their 1706 house, which is next to a Revolutionary War graveyard.

Each spring Marge waits hopefully for her crocuses, daffodils, and lilacs to bloom. The year runners and spectators trampled her plants, she got very angry, and when the runners left her yard littered she was even angrier. She fumed to George, who complained to a Hopkinton selectman, who responded by putting George on the town's Marathon committee. On the committee, George got to know the members of the B.A.A., especially race technical director Dave McGillivray. Gradually, problems were solved, and a long and warm relationship between the West family and the Boston Marathon began.

The Wests' house was the Valentine Tavern in the 18th century.

Three of the West's four children have run in the race. One year, their son brought his entire running team down from Maine to stay at the conveniently located family homestead. In recent years, the Wests have opened up their home to runners from Louisiana, one of whom introduced the West family to the joys of Cajun cooking.

START
135 E Main St.
HOPKINTON

Hopkinton Lemonade

A little boy named John Kelly and his brother grew up on the edge of the Hopkinton Common. One Marathon day, they cajoled their parents into buying them the ingredients for lemonade, and they set up a stand on the Common. Another year, their Boy Scout troop gathered to sell hot dogs. Their parents, Rick and Beth Kelly, held a rummage sale and hosted a Marathon day party at their house, which is directly on the bend in the road reached by the race leaders five seconds after the gun.

The family invited TV crews in for food and over the years they developed friendships with the regulars. One special year, famed broadcaster Howard Cosell came and stood on a platform high above the Common in front of their house.

One year, the boys jumped in and ran a few miles, but they have never run the whole thing. As an adult, John returned to the family home and resolved to train to run the Marathon. His sister plans to run, too. John Kelly said, about the race and living in Hopkinton, "It's like living at the bottom of a mountain and not climbing it . . . eventually you have to go to the top."

The arrival of thousands of people on the Hopkinton town green is a golden opportunity for entrepreneurs of all ages.

Through the years, Boy Scouts and other civic groups have held fund raisers and helped out.

Toll Boost

The Boston Marathon itself is a nonprofit event, but for the Massachusetts Turnpike Authority, the Marathon is more than profitable: it is a windfall. Ordinarily traffic is light on Monday holidays, but on Marathon day an extra 12,000 vehicles come through the Hopkinton tollbooth.

The Marathon is a windfall for the city of Boston in general. The influx of runners, press, and spectators in recent years spent upwards of $130 million, according to the Greater Boston Convention and Visitors Bureau.

Did you know?

A total of 45,978 vehicles and tolls of $62,911.95 on Patriots Day 1995 are compared to 33,785 vehicles and tolls of $53,479.60 on Memorial Day.

The Fitness Test

Once upon a time, the entire field of runners for the Boston Marathon dressed for the race in one farmhouse. Through the thirties, the Tebeau family opened their house to the marathoners, who covered the entire downstairs with their belongings and themselves. The whole house reeked of various liniments—wintergreen, witch hazel, and other substances—as runners sprawled around the house, each engaged in his own prerace ritual.

One prerace ritual was the physical. Since it was believed that a marathon was potentially harmful, only the most fit young men were allowed to run. Doctors examined each man, weighed him, listened to his heartbeat, and pronounced him fit enough or not to risk the run to Boston. In 1900, when the practice of fitness exams first began, the *Boston Herald* reported, "No weaklings will be permitted to start in the marathon tomorrow."

In 1958, doctors declared three runners unfit to race. They ran regardless and all finished in the top 10. Gradually it became understood that the human body is not only capable of running 26 miles, but generally benefits greatly from exercise of all kinds. The prerace fitness exams were discontinued in the sixties.

Race-day medical exams were once required for all competitors.

Did you know?

The Lucky Rock

The Lucky Rock marked the location of the Tebeau farm in Hopkinton where the Marathon field assembled and started in the thirties. The farm is now gone and the rock moved for highway expansion. The location is presently occupied by Weston Nurseries.

The Lucky Rock in 1929.

A Debt to Nature Due

As race day crowds press into the starting area, the elite runners are sequestered in the basement of the nearby First Congregational Church. Just before race time, the runners are led through a gate in the adjacent graveyard to their reserved starting area.

This old graveyard offers a somber contrast to the colorful pageantry outside its gates. There, under the cool shade of big trees, the nervous athletes walk respectfully over the mossy ground.

One grave they pass belongs to Lydia Perry. She died in the spring of 1817 at age 21, along with her younger brother, Jeduthun Perry. The runners, with their minds on the upcoming contest, do not stop to read the names on the lichen-covered slate stones. But if they did, they could read the words carved on the boy's stone: "Death is a debt to nature due. As I have paid it so must you."

Minutes before the start, the top runners walk silently through this graveyard.

Kenyans at School

It has become a tradition among schoolchildren in Hopkinton that on the Thursday before the Boston Marathon, the Kenyan runners visit their school. In the auditorium, the school band greets them with the Kenyan national anthem. A spotlight picks up the runners emerging from a patch of stage fog. The 600 middle school children cheer, impressed that they are in the company of the best runners in the world.

Kenyan marathoner Cosmas Ndeti takes time to visit schoolchildren.

The athletes and the students then break up into small groups to discuss their differing lives. Sammy Nygangincha describes his childhood: "When I woke up in Kenya, I would take up my books to run to school. I also had to run home for lunch, then back, and back home again." His teammate Gilbert Rutto added, "The accomplishments of the Kenyan National team inspired me to take up the sport." The 13 Kenyan athletes have been made honorary citizens of Hopkinton.

BURFOOT AND THE BOMB

Amby Burfoot, the 1968 Boston Marathon winner, returned to Boston in April of 2013 to race the course yet another time. At age 66, Burfoot didn't want to be anywhere else in the world on Patriots Day but on the Boston course. The race had fascinated him the first time he ran, as a teenager, with its pageantry and importance. Now the pilgrimage had become his custom. In the tradition of seven-time winner Clarence DeMar, two-time winner John A. Kelley, and Burfoot's coach and mentor John J. Kelley, who won in 1957, he wanted to come back again and again. The Boston Marathon is more than a footrace. It is a celebration of springtime in a pagan sense, and held on Patriots Day; it is a celebration of the American Revolution—the birth of freedom.

It had been 45 years since Burfoot's victory, which had come at a great expense of training and trepidation. Burfoot was a 21 year-old college student at the time who was confident that he would take the lead in the marathon and push the pace up the Newton Hills. He had spent a two-week spring break in March running a marathon a day, 175 miles a week. He felt power and confidence on that hot day 45 years earlier, but with the lead he also felt a sudden terror that all his competition could see him, but he could not see them. The hidden enemy lurked behind him and could sprint past at any time. Glory and fear drove him. It is not easy to run a marathon, but it is a thousand times harder to win one.

> **At age 66, Burfoot still wanted to be nowhere else in the world on Patriots Day but on the course for Boston.**

In contrast, on a pleasant day for running in 2013, Burfoot and friends trotted along in celebration. He paused in Wellesley at Wellesley College to collect kisses from coeds. In 1968, as much as he may have wanted to kiss and be kissed, he sped by at five minutes a mile, but this year in celebration he paused to gather congratulatory smooches. No hurry. No fear of competitors, most of whom were hours ahead. This was his homecoming, his party. Enjoy.

He and his friends expected to finish in about four and a half hours, out of the third wave. The contenders had finished two hours earlier, as Burfoot and company triumphantly entered Kenmore Square with a mile to go. It was 2:50 PM, or 4:09:43 since the start of the race, when everything changed.

Lining the finish area, people waited to see friends and family members finish. They wanted to celebrate, too. The top runners had finished their press conference in the Fairmont Copley Hotel ballroom and wandered with reporters in the corridors looking for food and drink—mostly with the runners looking for food and the reporters looking for drink. Police and officials who had been diligent about crowd control had relaxed as the crowds thinned. A couple of blocks away, the first explosion near the finish line, and then another, scattered spectators. Some lay injured on the sidewalk. Other people thought the explosions and smoke had been planned as part of the festivities, like fireworks. Suddenly police and others who had military experience knew the explosions came from bombs. They rushed toward the injured. They found carnage. The bombs, fashioned out of kitchen pressure cookers and left in backpacks on the sidewalk, killed three spectators—eight-year-old Martin Richards, twenty-three-year-old Boston University student Lu Lingzi, and twenty-nine-year-old restaurant manager Krystle Campbell. The bombs injured 264 people. A medical tent full of doctors and emergency medical technicians waited in the epicenter of the most medically equipped city in the world. Doctors, police, bystanders, and a few knowledgeable runners rushed to the wounded and applied their expertise to stop bleeding and save lives within minutes. Four-teen people would require amputations. Ambulances whisked the injured to 27 hospitals. Boston had been exquisitely prepared. Police and political leaders shut down the city.

A couple of blocks away, the first explosion near the finish line, and then another, scattered spectators. Some lay injured on the sidewalk. Other people thought the explosions and smoke had been planned as part of the festivities, like fireworks.

Officials shut down the marathon. Runners intent on finishing—their singular objective for the past four hours—suddenly heard shouts of "Stop!" instead of cheers of "Go!" Burfoot and friends saw crowds of people on the route ahead of them. Burfoot remembered the poor crowd control of the race back in the '60s and '70s when crowds leaned in to see the runners, leaving only a single path, and parted only slightly. Burfoot grew angry and annoyed that some drunken college students were blocking the road, ruining his race with their revelry. But as he ran closer, he saw they were runners, not drunks. Then his phone rang. It was his wife. "There's been an explosion at the finish line. The race is over. Don't try to keep running. Get back to the hotel." He obeyed. His race and that of thousands behind him ended.

But the race had only started for law enforcement and medical responders. In a great arc around the spot, that like in another city would be called ground zero, trained medical personnel rushed to help the wounded and protect everyone from any possible additional attacks. Emergency vehicles filled the streets as police evacuated everyone else. Information became rare and often wrong. In this fog of war, responders worked with incomplete information. Were they bombs? Gas explosions? Fireworks? Reports came in that a bomb had exploded at the Kennedy Library five miles away. No such thing had happened.

In this fog of war, responders worked with incomplete information. Were they bombs? Gas explosions? Fireworks?

At the Fairmont Copley Hotel, security guards shoved the reporters and athletes back into the building shouting, "Lockdown!" No explanation. The city, the subway, all shut down, block by block. Transportation shut down. Security controllers shut down cell towers to prevent cell phones from detonating any more bombs. The emergency departments of the hospitals filled up. The hotel stayed in lockdown for four hours.

Boston has many doctors. Some running in the marathon, such as Dr Natalie Stavas, sprinted to the wounded. Using a belt as a tourniquet to stop the bleeding, Stavas managed to save a woman whose leg had been ripped open by the blast. Stavas wished she could have done more. So many responders who ran toward the area where the bombs had exploded wished they could have done more but saw their duty to do everything they could, regardless of the possibility that yet other bombs would explode, adding them to the dead and injured. Any of the hundreds of abandoned bags could have had bombs in them ready to explode. They all had to be checked. But, people do what they are intent on doing, which is not so much heroic as human and automatic: if you can help, if you are there to help, if you know how to help, you do. And if you have come to Boston to finish a marathon, that is what you want to do, too.

Burfoot and others who were stopped a mile from their long-awaited and hard-earned finish line grew annoyed that something or someone had ruined what they had trained to accomplish. Most did not have phones.

In the Fairmont Copley lockdown, reporters, top runners, their agents, and their families crowded into the hotel bar. Mobile phones did not work. A big screen TV over the bar soundlessly played the same scene over and over of the marathon finish area shortly after the explosions as the ambulances arrived. Outside the windows of the bar, everyone could see the reflection of the flashing lights of police and medical vehicles in building windows, from around the corners. The only information came from the bartender's landline. He would repeat that the hotel and the blocks around it remained restricted to law-enforcement and medical personnel. The bartender reported that there had been explosions and people may be hurt. With plenty of food and drink and much company, people in the room alternated between feeling fear, being curious, and socializing. The reporters who usually had many words had no facts and little to say. They and the top runners chatted about other things, mostly the race that had become oddly unimportant, but had yet to be replaced with any specific understanding.

Only later would come the details of injury, of heroism, of the first responders rushing into insecure places where more bombs could be waiting. Only later would come the pain, the attempt to assuage it with charities such as One Fund that would collect $71.3 million for the injured and families of the dead. Tales of bravery and duty would fill the newspapers for the next year as the city and the nation tried to put the bombing into perspective.

Although Burfoot did not know exactly what had happened, he knew the marathon would never be the

same. All of Boston knew the marathon would never be the same. But all longed to be the same—unchanged, unmoved, strong. Denial would slowly turn to defiance.

As the story unfolded, the city became a ghost town

Although Burfoot did not know exactly what had happened, he knew the marathon would never be the same. All of Boston knew the marathon would never be the same.

and armed camp. Police hunted the suspects as they made a murderous escape, killing a police officer and carjacking a civilian. Transportation and business stopped. Police shot one alleged bomber in a military-style firefight. As the other hid, wounded, citizens rallied. The term "Boston Strong" began to appear everywhere and runners in the nationwide tribe of runners surged to qualify to race in the Boston Marathon of 2014.

Six months later the Boston Red Sox would win the World Series in a marathon tribute with the words "B. Strong" mowed into the outfield. The New York City marathon in solidarity painted a yellow line to their finish alongside the traditional blue line to match the traditional Boston Athletic Association colors.

The Boston Athletic Association that manages the race has opened it up to more qualifiers to satisfy the urge to defy, to pronounce Boston Strong, and to support and honor the victims and the courage of the first responders.

The urge seems to be one of defiance. "They can't stop me. They cannot stop Boston." These runners structure their lives to train, and in a metaphorical sense, run through the "wall", referring to the pain and depletion in the latter stages of a marathon race. They are people used to suffering but also used to

As the story unfolded, the city became a ghost town and armed camp. Police hunted the suspects as they made a murderous escape, killing a police officer and carjacking a civilian.

succeeding and overcoming difficulty. They are endurance athletes. They come back to try and try again. But the bombing brings a new trepidation. It's not of the difficulty of distance and pace, but a haunting question of what other act of horror could be pushed on the race. Will runners and spectators look with fear at every young man with a backpack? Will runners glance fearfully at rooftops and high windows fearing snipers? The two sides of a 26.2-mile road offer plenty of hiding places. There are only guesses about why someone may be driven to kill. What rationale cooks in the mind of someone who can kill uninvolved people for some political or religious cause? How can law enforcement, citizens, or runners themselves predict what may happen? The simplest explanation may be that people like those who planted the bombs first want to kill and only later justify it with some "cause." Might something similar happen again or never again? Runners will run, some in fear and defiance and others in hope and in celebration. The marathon will remain a soft target run by very hard people.

Regardless that the marathon could be a target for terrorists or demented people, Boston is physically and spiritually home. For residents, it is our Boston, our town. For marathon runners worldwide, the Boston Marathon is the premier marathon on the planet. Boston is the hometown of marathon racing. Other city marathons may be bigger or faster. Other marathons may offer Olympic gold medals in their ever-changing host cities, but Boston will always be home. Boston is the cradle of liberty. People fight for their homes, and after wars, hurricanes, earthquakes,

People emerge to rebuild. People do not want to leave their homes, just as marathon runners do not want to quit their race.

tsunamis, or tornados, people want to go home. Seldom have cities under siege warfare surrendered. The citizens of cities bombed to rubble redouble their resistance. They go underground. People emerge to rebuild. People do not want to leave their homes, just as marathon runners do not want to quit their race.

Amby Burfoot and tens of thousands of others want to come back. It is a homing instinct. It will be spring. It will be time to get to Boston.

Hopkinton Runners

JOE KAISER got a job in Sudbury, Massachusetts, in 1986. He chose to live in Hopkinton so he could train on the Marathon course and the quiet roads around town. The training has paid off. He had run the race 12 times before 1996.

LAURA ANDERSON loves the crowds along the Marathon route. She ran the marathon in each of the first two years after she moved to Hopkinton.

Hopkinton Runners

Hopkinton-raised JANE WELZEL grew up with the Boston Marathon, graduated from the University of Massachusetts, and ran her first road race ever in the Boston Marathon in 1975. By 1990, she was one of America's top women marathoners, qualifying for the Olympic Trials in Boston in 1984, 1988, and 1992.

JACK O'ROURKE lives in Hopkinton, a convenient 300 yards from the start. He has run the Marathon about 20 times. For 25 years, he taught English at Marian High School in Framingham and coached track.

ASHLAND

EXIT 12

9

3

FRAMINGHAM TRAIN DEPOT

ASHLAND CLOCK TOWER

ASHLAND

2

10K

8

7

6

Concord St

Union Ave

W Central St

Waverly St

5

1

4

Union St

STATE PARK

START LINE 1897-1923

W Union St

5K

3

Chestnut St

Concord St

Pond St

2

STYLIANOS KYRIAKIDES STATUE

START

1

E Main St

HOPKINTON

Highland

126

BOSTON MARATHON®
Official JetBlue Course Map

Ashland

Ashland was incorporated in 1846. It was once called Unionville and later referred to as "Clock Town." In 1916 Henry E. Warren invented the first self-starting electrical clock and called it the Telechron. True to marathoner doggedness, when Warren invented his clock, plugged it in, and found it did not keep good time, he kept at it. He traced the problem to the fact that the electricity varied. Electricity did not arrive at exactly 60 cycles per second, so Warren invented another device that corrected the problem. The Telechron put a lot of people to work during the Great Depression when the Ashland factory made up to 800,000 clocks per year. By the year 2000 the population of Ashland had reached 14,674.

The First Start

The start of the first Boston Marathon, on Patriots Day in 1897, was in Ashland, in front of Metcalf's Mill. The B.A.A. appointed double Olympic gold medalist Tom Burke to start the race. When Burke arrived at the start—having taken the train along with all the other officials, contestants, and their handlers—he found no starting line and, of course, was not aware of any tradition to start precisely at noon. So things got going a little late. Burke scratched a line in the dirt road with his foot and, having no gun (another tradition yet to come), merely shouted "Go." He did not have to shout loudly, since he faced only 15 men.

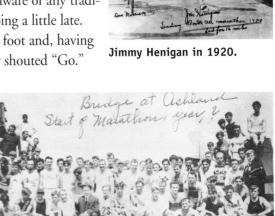

Jimmy Henigan in 1920.

Each man had a handler on a bicycle to ride alongside and see to his needs for water, food, massage, encouragement, and stimulants. The only man without a handler was Dick Grant, a miler who immediately took the lead but did not keep it. John J. McDermott overtook him later in the race and

The 1910 runners at the bridge in Ashland before the start.

won the first Boston Marathon. He had run a distance of about 24½ miles, finishing on the Irvington Street Oval during a track meet held near the B.A.A. clubhouse. The Oval, the track meet, and the B.A.A. clubhouse no longer exist.

An Extreme Sport

John J. McDermott, the first winner of the Boston Marathon, seems like a quaint and slow figure from the past. All we have of him is a rough line drawing from the 1897 *Boston Daily Globe*. But in fact McDermott was one of the hotshot athletes of his day.

Marathon racing was an infant sport. At that time, people knew nothing about training, human endurance, or cardiac capacity, but they regularly saw horses drop dead on the streets from exertion. So this novel form of racing was considered dangerous and difficult, but fascinating and admirable. The crowds gathered along the Marathon course to watch real men dare death to beat one another to Boston. These men were not running for their health, and they were regarded as death-defying daredevils.

John J. McDermott.

In the conventional wisdom of the time, young men were cautioned not to run more than one marathon in a lifetime because it was thought likely to lead to permanent heart damage. It was said that a marathon "uses a man up." McDermott ran the Boston Marathon a second time in 1898, then disappeared. No one knows what happened to him, how long he lived, or if the Marathon did in fact use him up.

The Shoving Match

A few miles into the 1967 Boston Marathon, Kathrine Switzer ran in the cold drizzle in the company of her coach and her boyfriend. She had gone to the starting line in a hooded sweatshirt like many others were wearing that damp day. Under it was an official B.A.A. starting number; she was the first woman to wear one. She doffed her hood and started with no officials noticing that No. #261 was a woman. But then the press bus passed the runners.

A sharp-eyed reporter noticed her and looked up her number next to the name K. Switzer in the program. He teased B.A.A. official Jock Semple, the crusty old Scotsman and self-appointed guardian of the race. "Hey, Jock, this K. Switzer looks pretty good."

Another reporter joined in, "What's her mother call her . . . Karl?"

In 1967 Jock Semple tried to retrieve K. Switzer's number.

Jock Semple did not take teasing well. He exploded in fury that some woman would jump into his race in defiance of the rules in order to make some feminist statement. Semple felt the race was for marathoners only and that social commentary belonged on the editorial pages of the newspapers. Race director Will Cloney agreed. Together they leaped off the bus with Semple leading the way, shouting, "Get the hell out of my race!"

Semple tried to get the number back. He felt it was B.A.A. property obtained by subterfuge. But Switzer's boyfriend intervened and sent Jock Semple sprawling. K. Switzer went on to finish in a flurry of press attention. It would be five more years before women were officially welcomed to race.

The Run for the Hoses

Jack Fultz did not come to Boston to win the Marathon in 1976. In fact, when he saw the weather, he didn't want to run at all. But he did want a qualifying time for the Olympic Trials to be held in Eugene, Oregon. With a time under 2:20, the Olympic Committee would pay an athlete's expenses to the trials. Stormy weather had prevented Fultz from getting his qualifying time earlier in the year. And this year a heat wave smothered Boston. But he had to run; Boston was his last chance.

So bad was the heat wave that someone affixed a sign to the front grille of the lead bus. It read: "Hose the Runners." Thus the race, which moved through towns where thermometers registered over 100°F, became known as "The Run for the Hoses."

Fultz started his run conservatively following 1968 winner Amby Burfoot and gradually passed one wilting runner after another. He tried to contain his excitement. Residents along the course read the sign on the bus and ran for their hoses. They rallied to wet the runners. Fultz ran sopping wet to first place and to victory. But with a time of 2:20:19, the stubborn Olympic Committee still would not pay his way.

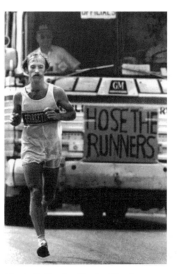

Jack Fultz in the hottest Marathon ever.

Clarence DeMar

Eighty-year-old Al Awad remembered in 1996 when he and his cousins were about twelve years old. They used to run up to Hopkinton to see Clarence DeMar and the start of the Marathon and then run home to Ashland.

Clarence H. DeMar was born in 1888. When he was 10 years old, his father died. His mother sent young Clarence off to the Boston Farm School on Thompson's Island in Boston Harbor. Young DeMar tried to escape the island with some other young boys by swimming through the harbor. They were caught and returned to the Farm School.

As a youth, DeMar proved to be a bookish loner, but when he got to the University of Vermont he discovered cross-country running. Like most boys, he wanted to find a sport at which he could excel—for DeMar, running was it. Quickly he learned that he was not a fast runner but he was willing to train more than anyone else.

He ran his first Boston Marathon in 1910, placing second. The next year he won. DeMar made the U.S. Olympic marathon team in 1912, 1920, and 1924, where he won the bronze medal. Altogether he won seven Boston Marathons—the record so far.

Clarence H. DeMar.

Dick and Rick Hoyt

Thirty-three-year-old Rick Hoyt has cerebral palsy that classifies him as a spastic quadriplegic. He cannot run or push his own wheelchair. When he was 16, he wanted to compete in a road race near his home. His 54-year-old father could run, so Rick suggested that his father could push him. They completed their 30th Boston Marathon in 2012, when Dick was 72 and Rick was 50.

Now Dick Hoyt pushes Rick Hoyt along the Boston Marathon course in a specially built carriage to raise public awareness about the disabled and money for his Hoyt fund, which promotes the integration and acceptance of persons with all types of disabilities into every aspect of society.

At the start of the Boston Marathon, the elder Hoyt leans his weight against the counterbalance of his son's vehicle and scoots to Boston with surprising speed. They start with the wheelchair racers. The crowd's reaction to the Hoyts' passage is galvanic. Cheers and good wishes follow them to Boston.

Rick and Dick Hoyt.

Leslie Pawson, Pawtucket

Les Pawson was highly respected as a gentleman as well as an athlete by all who knew him. He first swept into Boston Marathon history by winning the 1933 race by a large margin, despite a monster headwind, over Canadian Dave Komonen. That year Pawson was a textile mill worker.

In 1938, in the Great Depression, Pawson worked outdoors as foreman of groundskeepers of People's Park in Pawtucket, Rhode Island. Marathon day was a hot one, but Pawson defeated a strong field that included six former winners.

By the time he achieved his third victory in 1941, Pawson was serving as an alderman in Pawtucket and worked in a defense plant. It was another hot day. A reporter for the Boston Globe wrote, "His raven's wing hair was plastered in strings over his weatherbeaten face." During this race Pawson shared water with Johnny A. Kelley, and a long friendship developed between the two.

Pawson died at age 87 on October 13, 1992, in Pawtucket. An annual race is held in his honor in Lincoln, Rhode Island, each April.

Leslie Pawson (left) and Johnny Kelley (right) in 1938.

Ashland Runners

ELIZABETH BOGARDUS lived in Ashland for 12 years and ran an interior decorating business as well as the Marathon, which she ran 10 times. She grew up in Framingham and had always wanted to jump into the Marathon when she was a kid.

JOHN KIRK, an Ashland resident, grew up in Framingham and has watched the race roll by since childhood. He ran in 1994, despite being diabetic. He had lots of friends along the course who stationed themselves at three-mile intervals to supply him with sugar so he could "be a part of the rich history of the race."

Master Bandit Peter Foley

In 1910 the B.A.A. told Peter Foley, a 52-year-old diamond cutter from Winchester, Massachusetts, that he was too old to run the race. It was thought that the marathon was a young man's race and that men with long gray beards like Foley's might damage themselves. Foley wanted to run anyway, so he shaved off his whiskers and jumped into the race. The B.A.A. officials saw only a smooth-faced man in good shape. Thus Peter Foley became the first bandit in the race. Years later, the Masters Division was formed for older runners.

Another convention held that the only reason to enter a race was to have a chance to win. Before Peter Foley, all entrants considered themselves contenders. Foley, however, ran a fairly slow race and was the first to enter with no intention of trying to win. Now only one out of a hundred entrants attempts to win. It is acceptable to enter the race to run a personal record time or to place as high as possible. Thousands now run to celebrate the race by gracefully touring the course, thousands who can trace their participation back to hoary old Foley.

Did you know?

In the 1995 race, 350,000 paper cups were used for about 40,000 gallons of water and Gatorade. Also used were 284 portable toilets. And 200 buses.

TEAM COMPETITION

Serious declared teams from all over the country compete to win the Boston Marathon team prize. They also look very good in formal evening attire. The top three runners from the same club score for their team. A team may enter as many as 15 runners in one of four divisions: open men, open women, masters men, and masters women. The teams score by accumulated time. In 2013, the Boston Athletic Association (the host team) won the men's team prize with a time of 7 hours 12 minutes and 19 seconds. That meant that three men who live

In the women's race, Dirigo Running Club, based in Maine, beat the host B.A.A. by 2 minutes, or 40 seconds per runner. Sheri Piers led the Maine team with a 2:39:25. From 1985 to 2013, the host B.A.A. men's team won the team title eight times, and their women's team won nine times. In the masters men's team competition, the Greater Lowell (MA) Road Runners have won eight times since 1992, and the nearby Whirlaway Racing team has won seven times. Whirlaway masters women dominated the race in 2010, 2011, and 2012.

The teams receive their prizes—beautiful Waterford Crystal bowls etched with the place and year—at the swanky, exclusive awards ceremony in the Grand Ballroom in the Fairmont Copley Plaza hotel on the evening after the race. At the glittering formal ceremony, the top athletes, B.A.A. officials, and Boston dignitaries, all in evening dress, applaud as the winners receive their awards looking nothing like the sweaty athletes they were a few hours earlier.

At the glittering formal ceremony, the top athletes, B.A.A. officials, and Boston dignitaries, all in evening dress, applaud as the winners receive their awards looking nothing like the sweaty athletes they were a few hours earlier.

near each other and train and race together averaged under 2:25 per marathon. Tim Richie, who has raced a mile under four minutes, led the team with a 2:21:31.

FRAMINGHAM

FRAMINGHAM

NATI

9

LAKE
COCHITUATE

135

3

8

15K

10

9

FRAMINGHAM
TRAIN DEPOT

2

7

W Central St

Union Ave

Concord St

Speen St

S Main St

10K

6

Waverly St

ASHLAND
CLOCK TOWER

5

27

1

4

Union St

Concord St

Chestnut St

Pond St

STYLIANOS
KYRIAKIDES
STATUE

BOSTON MARATHON®
Official JetBlue Course Map

jetBlue

FRAMINGHAM

NEWTON

NATICK

HALF

BROOKLINE

WELLESLEY

BOSTON

FINISH

ASHLAND

START

HOPKINTON

Framingham

With almost 67,000 people and a bustling downtown in South Framingham, which is where the Marathon passes through, Framingham is a big town. Although bigger than some cities, it has a town government. Framingham is full of industry and commerce and, like a city, is home to a mixture of ethnic groups. If there is a city of big shoulders on the Marathon route, Framingham is it.

The Happy Swallow

The Happy Swallow is a bar in Framingham. "It is the biggest day of the year for us," said Pete Phylis, the owner for 34 years before selling it and retiring in 2011. He saw the same people run by every year and had special words of encouragement for his regulars who run the race. The Happy Swallow tavern was established in 1937 and does 30 percent more business on Marathon day than on any other day of the year.

Pete's favorite story? One year a Marathon runner stopped in for a happy swallow from a tavern mug. He ran out the door, ran a block, turned around, ran back to the Happy Swallow, and ordered something stronger. He didn't leave until closing.

Marathon day is the busiest day of the year for the Happy Swallow.

Paul Revere's Ride

If the Boston Marathon commemorates Patriots Day and the Battle of Lexington on April 19, 1775, why doesn't it follow the route of Paul Revere's famous ride?

The original designers of the B.A.A. marathon course, John Graham and Herbert H. Holton, did consider Paul Revere's ride and tried to lay out a course from Lexington to Boston, but there were problems.

Paul Revere was not the only one who spread the word that the Redcoats were coming. Many riders had been appointed to alarm the countryside. One unknown rider rode north through Medford, Woburn, and Wilmington all the way to Tewksbury. William Dawes rode the southern loop through Roxbury and Brighton. Martin Herrick rode through Stoneham. These riders met other riders and set off the alarm in a relay.

The problem that Graham and Holton faced in 1896 was, which route? The roads had changed greatly since 1775. No one knew the routes in detail and ones that were known weren't long enough. However, the railroad west led to Ashland station and ran parallel to a road back to Boston. It was a logical choice and thus became the Marathon route.

Sheet music cover for "Paul Revere's Ride."

Music on the Roof

When Silvano Melchiorri of Natick heard the Marathon coming, he took his band up on the roof of R. H. Long's Cadillac dealership in Framingham. He took up the tuba player, the bass player, the snare drummer, the clarinetist, the trombonist, the banjo player, and, most important, the trumpeter. When the runners came into sight, the band began to play their unique Italian/Dixieland music. The spectators loved it. They gathered around the building and sang along, changing the words from "When the saints go marching in" to "When the runners come running in."

This brought grins from the runners. Some stopped to take pictures. One said, "I look forward to it . . . it gives me that extra jolt." Some runners even paused to dance in the streets.

Silvano Melchiorri's Dixieland Hobos up on the roof.

Did you know?

No Sweat?

If 25,000 runners run the Marathon on a hot day and each one sweats away 10 pounds, that's about 31,000 gallons of sweat.

Waiting for a Freight Train

In the 1907 race the top 10 runners crossed the train tracks in Framingham with race favorite Tom Longboat among them. In the next group was Bob Fowler. His experience with the Marathon had led him to run slowly over the early miles and save his energy for the closing miles. He wanted very much to win and had trained carefully, working very hard.

Longboat heard the train coming and couldn't help chuckling to himself. When Fowler got to the railroad track, a slow freight train blocked his path. His competition ran away ahead of him while he fumed for one minute and 15 seconds. Everyone from 300 yards behind caught up.

After the train passed, Fowler blasted off, but he failed to catch Longboat. Fowler finished second with a running time that would have won many Boston Marathons.

Framingham Runners

RICH CHESMORE lives two-tenths of a mile off the course in Framingham. He trains on the course almost every day. He was also the women's cross-country coach at Framingham State College. In 1983 he ran the course in a respectable 2:35.

SEAN ROSKEY grew up in Framingham, ran track in high school there, and graduated to track and cross-country at the Naval Academy. As a child, he stood with his father handing out orange slices during the Marathon. The elder Roskey decided to run the race himself, and Sean joined him. Eventually Sean ran officially, with a 2:44:55 finish, in 1995.

Running Clubs Volunteer

The members of several local running clubs volunteer their expertise to the Boston Marathon. On race day, they assist the press in covering the race. Many also host the visiting elite runners in the days before the race.

Fifty members of the Greater Framingham Track Club, led by Loni Townley, watch all the official digital checkpoint clocks along the course. There are 32 timing stations along the route.

Thirty members of the Greater Lowell Road Runners, coordinated by Ernie Roy, operate the prerace number pick-up. Other running clubs, including the Merrimack Valley Striders and Central Mass Striders, lend a hand. Since they know the sport, they don't have to be trained.

Student runners from Winthrop High School hand out fluids to runners. Students from Governor Dummer Academy—an international private school—help with language translations at the international athlete number pick-up tables. Track and cross-country teams from Wellesley College work at the pasta party, and teams from Stonehill College and Salem University also volunteer.

B. A. A.

He Died Running

Jimmy Duffy was a lively, talkative runner who won the Boston Marathon in 1914. He outran fellow Canadian Edouard Fabre and vowed he would return the next year to defend his title. But world events would not have it.

War had broken out in Europe, and Canada quickly joined England in trench warfare against Germany. Jimmy Duffy volunteered for service and traveled with the 16th Battalion to Ypres. There, on a mid-April night, his squad was ordered to charge a German machine gun emplacement.

The Germans sent up a flare to light the hillside. The glare and the machine guns caught Jimmy Duffy running full sprint to attack. He died almost a year after his Boston victory.

Statue of an unidentified doughboy.

The Day the Tar Melted

The weather isn't always nice for the Boston Marathon. In fact, New England has a perverse habit of un-nice weather. To further complicate matters, weather that is good for spectators—warm and sunny—is bad for running fast times.

In 1909 the Boston Marathon had its first "inferno" when temperatures exceeded 83°F and a little-known cotton mill worker from New Hampshire named Henri Renaud ran from 53rd place in Framingham past dilapidated and dehydrated runners to victory.

In 1927, when the technology of paving roads was still in its infancy, the heat of the day melted the tar on the roads. The hot, sticky tar clung to the soles of the runners' shoes, and 35 men dropped out of the race in the first mile. By seven miles, the course record holder and defending champion Johnny Miles quit with his feet fried to blisters.

In 1952, another cotton mill worker, this time from Guatemala, seemed unaffected by high temperatures. Doroteo Flores won by a huge margin.

But the hottest Marathon day came in 1976, when temperatures topped 100°F at some points along the course. Jack Fultz won that race, which they dubbed "The Run for the Hoses." The lead bus carried a sign that read "Hose the runners," and the community responded with water in all ways.

Other years have been exceptionally cold. In 1925, flurries of snow blew in the runners' faces. Winner Chuck Mellor stuffed that day's newspaper into the front of his shirt to break the wind. In 1933, a cold headwind off the North Atlantic turned winner Les Pawson's arms lobster red. In 1967, a scum of slushy snow covered the lawns in Hopkinton on the day of the race.

It has also rained many times. In 1939, Ellison "Tarzan" Brown won in the pouring rain, as did Ron Hill in 1970.

The fastest running day was in 2011. The race has never been canceled because of weather.

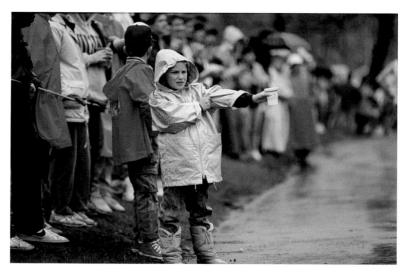

Helping out in the rain.

The Olympic Jinx

For the longest time, Olympic champions came to Boston as heavy favorites and failed to win. It seemed there was a jinx against Olympic gold medalists winning the Boston Marathon.

In the first decade of the century, champions John Hayes and Bill Sherring failed to win in Boston but did win the Olympic gold. In 1926, the Finnish runner Albin Stenroos came to Boston a heavy favorite after his marathon gold in the Paris Olympics in 1924, but young upstart Johnny Miles outran him.

Delfo Cabrera from Argentina came with the gold he earned in 1948 in London but finished sixth in the 1954 Boston Marathon.

Olympic champion Abebe Bikila of Ethiopia came to Boston in 1963 to face a field that had virtually conceded the race to him. But after leading the first half, the vicissitudes of the course did in the Olympic champion and left him staggering in a cold rain as the rest of the field passed him by.

The 1972 Olympic gold medalist, Frank Shorter, came to Boston twice and placed dismally: 23rd and 75th.

In 1983 Joan Benoit won Boston in a world record and went on to the Los Angeles Olympics to win. But still no runner already holding an Olympic gold medal won the Boston Marathon. The press called Boston the Graveyard of Olympic Champions.

It was not until 1990 that a remarkable pair of runners smashed the jinx. That year the winners of both the men's and women's Olympic marathon gold medals came to Boston and won: Gelindo Bordin and Rosa Mota.

Gelindo Bordin.

Rosa Mota.

Did you know?

Horse on the Course

Horse trainers say that a well-trained horse, such as Paul Revere's Brown Beauty, could gallop the Boston Marathon course in less than an hour. So far none has done so.

Natick

Natick is the community surrounding Lake Cochituate. Granted a charter in 1650, it was at that time an Indian community, home to the Narraganset tribe. At the outbreak of King Philip's War in 1675, the British colonists imprisoned the Indians on Deer Island in Boston Harbor. Most of them died on the island. Centuries later, Ellison "Tarzan" Brown, a descendant of King Philip, led the Marathon twice through Natick on his way to victory in the thirties.

Now Natick, with its 32,000 residents, is a comfortable town just beyond the grip of Greater Boston. It is home to the sprawling U.S. Army Laboratories, where pioneering research has continued since World War II.

Volunteers

Volunteers often do the same job year after year and get quite good at it. They work with the same people, form friendships, and agree to meet again, same time, next year. Dr. William Castelli has worked in the medical tent for 18 years. Others, led by Jim D'Angelo, stay for trash detail. Their identification badges, marked "TRASH," provoke some fun. One serious job of volunteers is to guard the mile markers so they will not be stolen by souvenir hunters.

For a hard day's work, the volunteers get an official Boston Marathon jacket, a pin, an invitation to the postrace party, and, for the finish line workers, a bag lunch.

More people volunteer to help with the Boston Marathon than there are jobs for them to do. In 1995, volunteer coordinator Marilynn Bright had to turn away 700 volunteers. She has organized 103 team captains to do all the jobs. The volunteers start at the crack of dawn and are still at it late into the evening.

Bricklayer Bill Kennedy and the Ancient Marathoners

As the men who ran the marathon aged, they noticed that their physical prowess remained quite high. Moreover, they liked running marathons. So after the first decade of the Boston Marathon, each era to follow had its ancient marathoner.

"Bricklayer" Bill Kennedy, who won the Boston Marathon in 1917, came back to run a total of 28 times by 1941. He started the tradition of the ancient marathoner. He worked as a mason and took temporary jobs where races were scheduled as a way to finance his travel.

Clarence H. DeMar continued the tradition. DeMar ran the Boston Marathon 33 times. The last time he ran was in 1954 when he was 65. That year he ran 3:58. DeMar set the standard for Kelley.

John Adelbert Kelley ran the Boston Marathon 61 times from 1928 to 1992. He started at age 20 and stopped at age 84. He won the Marathon twice, placed second seven times, and was in the top 10 17 times.

Not many runners have exceeded DeMar, but several plan to. Ben Beach of Maryland has run 28 in a row. Neil Wygandt from Pennsylvania has run more. John J. Kelley, the 1957 winner, has run about 30, but not consecutively. Perfect records of all the finishers were not recorded in the early years, so we cannot be sure who has run the most Marathons in a row.

But we are sure no one has run as many as the elder Kelley. Three-time winner Cosmas Ndeti says he wants Johnny A. Kelley's record, which will take until the year 2054, but Ndeti never returned to Boston.

THE MARATHON AND MODERN MEMORY

More than any other Olympic running event, the marathon is an event of memory. It creates a memory of the course itself with unique geology, geography, and culture. Each road, and each street, is unlike any other. The marathon memorializes a victory over Persian armies in 490 BC that, as modern memory goes, saved European civilization from defeat by people who are now called Iranians. The memory contained in the marathon has changed in the minds of current participants and spectators. No longer is it one man's sacrifice for country; it has morphed into other kinds of memories.

With so many people running so many marathons, the recollected history of the marathon is changing faster than ever.

New research tells us that memories are not scratched into clay and baked to be preserved forever. Rather, they are malleable. Memories change as they are revisited, to help in the remembering body's survival. Memories recalled more frequently change more than those that are seldom recalled. With so many people running so many marathons, the recollected history of the marathon is changing faster than ever.

Clarence DeMar, nicknamed Mister DeMarathon, who won the event seven times, experienced a profound change in his mind regarding the meaning of racing a marathon. He won in 1911 and did not win again until 1922. In the intervening years he held doubts in his mind of the propriety of self-aggrandizing. DeMar felt that racing and winning the marathon called too much attention to himself. He called the pursuit of the marathon "vainglorious." Strict amateur standards contained the marathon in amateur straits, preventing it from becoming a means to earning a living which essentially kept the poorer classes out of noble competition. A common sense at that time held that a person should not brag about himself. Early literature about the marathon, especially DeMar's autobiography, showed his attempt to set personal aggrandizement behind a larger idea. In the first half of the 20th century few books appeared making the runner into a hero. Such attention to winners and their sacrifice fit the motif of the marathon as a tribute to heroic sacrifice. For many decades, the marathon racers seemed to be the "guests" of the host club. The sponsoring B.A.A. charged no entry fee. It would be a while before the runner became a customer and began to think like a customer. But with growing numbers of runners, change came suddenly.

The shock came with the publication of a book by Jim Fixx in 1977: *The Complete Book of Running*, which glorified mere participation. That was the point when health and fitness participation caught up to personal heroic sacrifice in an attempt to win. No longer did the entrant start a marathon with the intention to win, try to win, or race as well as possible and accept the humble consequent of some degree of loss, but instead everyone became a winner.

On the 1967 Boston Marathon entry blank some notifications to the runner would seem odd to contemporary marathon runners. (The 1967 marathon was the author's first marathon the month he turned 18.)

First it was called the American Marathon Run, with trophies to the first 10 men and medals to the next 25. An engraved finishing place number on the back of each medal gave it unique meaning. Also, scoring for the team prize appeared on the entry blank: "A special trophy will be awarded to the club whose first three athletes to finish score the least number of points. The system will be as follows: first place counts one; second place, two; third place three, etc.)". No mention of an entry fee appeared on the blank. The results reported the athlete's name and club, not his city or town of residence. By 1975 the

top 100 runners received medals. Some time later all finishers received medals, not at a prize ceremony, but at the finish line. Also, the entry fee began its steady climb while finishing times became slower and slower. In the early days the officials left the finish area about four hours after the start.

In 1967 when Kathrine Switzer finished in about 4:20, officials had gone home. (They were present to note that Roberta Gibb finished in 3:27:17.). From the '60s to the '70s, runners changed from exclusively competing athletes to customers, listed as if for marketing purposes, by town of origin. With so many finishers, place became meaningless. The runners began to think like customers and demand more amenities such as medals for all finishers. Why not? They had paid for them.

In 1981, Terry Fox, having had one leg amputated due to cancer, attempted to run across Canada to raise awareness for cancer research. He ran the equivalent of a marathon a day on one real leg and one artificial leg. He did not complete his journey. Cancer spread to his lungs, so he had to abandon his cross-continent run, and died nine months later. His sacrifice brought a new notion to the idea of the marathon and sacrifice. Now the marathon, by sacrifice of runners, raises millions of dollars for organizations such as Dana-Farber Cancer Institute, Alzheimer's Association, and dozens more. Runners may earn a Boston entry now without running a qualifying time if they raise a sum of money such as $5,000 to $8,000 each. The idea of heroism changed.

New runners entered the race with not even a dream of winning, but with an important personal quest. They moved on from marathon day with their own, new personal memories and stories. Shaped by the books and words of Dr. George A. Sheehan, runners sought an inner meaning. Sheehan was a cardiologist whose first book, *Dr. Sheehan on Running*, appeared in 1975 and last published after his death in 1993 called, *Going the Distance: One Man's Journey to the End of His Life*, which powerfully signaled a turn inward to explore the runner's mind. Perhaps his most influential book was *Running & Being: The Total Experience* in 1978. Dr. Sheehan gave legitimacy to the "every runner" experience in the marathon. Now runners trained for and entered a marathon not to see how they could do, but what they could feel and reveal about their inner selves. Sheehan raced up to his dying days as competitively as he could. Before one race, he said to a fellow competitor, as casually as one would mention a sore muscle before a race, "I haven't been able to train as much as I should because of this cancer."

An ultimate introspective book about running may be the perfectly titled, *What I Talk About When I Talk About Running* by Haruki Murakami. One quotation from the book illustrates a new kind of thinking about one's achievements: "For a runner like me,

what's really important is reaching the goal I set myself, under my own power. I give it everything I have, endure what needs enduring, and am able, in my own way, to be satisfied." In Clarence DeMar's era one would not declare in public that one had a right in his own way to say he is satisfied. A man in 1920 would not say he is proud of himself. That would be for others to say.

Films about running have evolved in a similar way to rapidly revised modern memory of the marathon. The 1962 film *The Loneliness of the Long Distance Runner*, based on Alan Sillitoe's short story, tells of a champion runner who forgoes personal victory on principle. Few people now would celebrate a character taking material loss for a higher principle especially when that decision produces no fame. The 1978 made-for-television movie, *See How She Runs*, is the story of a 40-year-old divorced teacher whose life is changed by her decision to enter the Boston Marathon. In 1994, in the movie *Forrest Gump*, the titular character runs to purge the demons within. Forrest Gump ran for three years, 14 days, and 16 hours as personal catharsis to put the memory of a personal relationship behind him. Running seemed in the public mind to have become a drug for self-realization, perhaps like LSD and other hallucinogens.

In Jon Dunham's documentaries about the marathon, *Spirit of the Marathon I* and *Spirit of the Marathon II*, the characters followed are vastly different runners and unique characters, from professionals to the extraordinarily average runners. In the films, the average runners steal the show from the professionals. There is also the story of the woman whose father died of pancreatic cancer and in whose memory she will run the depicted marathon (Rome) as the first of her 52 marathons in a year to raise money for pancreatic cancer awareness. Here is depicted personal sacrifice and heroism in personal memory and

> **"For a runner like me, what's really important is reaching the goal I set myself, under my own power. I give it everything I have, endure what needs enduring, and am able, in my own way, to be satisfied."**

in pain. So much of marathon running has become about "causes," charities, and raising awareness. But such awareness raised is exactly what Clarence DeMar would call "vainglorious."

The height of self-reference rather than self-sacrifice can be seen in the runner who runs in the Boston Marathon wearing a shirt with his or her own name on it. What could have migrated further from the idea of ancient Pheidippides shouting with his last breath, "Rejoice, WE (not I) conquer," or the words on the tomb of the unknown soldier—known only to God.

On April 15, 2013, however, the bombings suddenly sparked the memory of the marathon as a militant act of defiance and jarred it back to its origins. More people than ever want to run the marathon in 2014 to remember the sacrifice of the people killed and injured in the bombing and to honor and thank the first responders. The concept of duty seems to have returned alongside, if not replacing, the concepts of fitness, self-realization, and self-congratulation. Again runners remember with reverence the symbolism of duty, of giving, of life and death, of the events of April 15, 2013, and the exact place...

Oddballs

Jock Semple and Will Cloney, the guardians of the Boston Marathon through its middle years, feared that the race would attract "the nuts." There were people who came for reasons other than running a footrace. Some have run espousing various causes, others to get in the newspapers.

Many have merely wanted attention, and each of these clowns had his own act. Jimmy "Cigars" Connors ran the course in the thirties with 26 cigars in his hands—one to smoke for each mile.

Local college fraternities sometimes charged their pledges to jump in at the end and sprint with the winner. Such attention-getting antics infuriated Semple and Cloney. They wanted nothing to take away from the glory of the winner of the race.

The race now has stronger management and more security, and the "nuts" can be kept separate from the racers. The crowds view the nuts as part of the fun. Cowman X ran with a horned cow's head on top of his head. There is a Groucho Marx. One year, comedian Pat Paulsen took several days to complete the course, holding an umbrella. Comedian Dick Gregory ran once as part of a symbolic protest. Then there's the guy with a beer can suspended on a stick and dangling in front of his head. He doesn't get it until he reaches the finish line.

"Groucho Marx."

Shins with a message.

Natick Runners

JUDITH OXFORD has run five times. Now a federal proba-
tion officer, she grew up on West Central Street in Natick
full of dreams to run the Boston Marathon. She began
training and built up to 60 to 70 miles per week. Her co-
workers said she'd never make it, but she showed them. She
ran the course in 1993 in 3:30. She says, "I feel so con-
nected; it changed my outlook."

NICK COSTES, a sixth-grade teacher in Natick, finished
ninth, third, and fourth in the mid-fifties. He is a Boston
University graduate and was a teammate of John J. Kelley.
In the 1955 race, he wore a Natick High School track singlet, and his students cheered him through the town.

Go Jump in the Lake

In the early years of the Boston Marathon, Jerry Nason was its perennial reporter for the *Boston Globe*. He told a lot of the Marathon's most enduring stories. He claimed that as an infant his nurse held him up to the window of a hospital in Newton to watch the marathoners run by in 1909 when he was five days old, and that since then he'd never missed a Boston Marathon. He named Heartbreak Hill.

Nason always had an ear for a good story. One he picked up from Fred Brown, of the North Medford running club, concerned the Narraganset Indian Ellison "Tarzan" Brown, who had won the race. With tongue in cheek, Fred told Nason that one year during the race Tarzan had jumped into Lake Cochituate in Natick and liked the cool water so much he stayed. Although it never happened, it was considered plausible and it made a good story. Nason told it and retold it. The Marathon is like that—myth becomes bigger than life.

Runners passing Lake Cochituate.

Widest Margins of Victory

Men—6:52 in 1897 John J. McDermott over James J. Kiernan

Women—9:59 in 1972 Nina Kuscsik over Elaine Pederson

Smallest Margins of Victory

Men—less than 1 second in 2000 Elijah Lagat over Gezahegne Abere

Women—1 second in 2009 Salina Kosgei over Dire Tune

Cosmas Ndeti

Cosmas Ndeti trained in his hometown of Machakos, Kenya, with his boyhood friend Benson Masya. Although a serious trainer and racer, as well as being deeply religious, Ndeti can make a good joke. One day he and his friend shaved their heads and so became known around town as the two coconuts. When his agent called collect from a European airport to say he needed money because his luggage, wallet, everything had been stolen, Ndeti suggested that they just send a guitar and a tin cup and let him earn his way back.

On the weekend in 1993 when Ndeti won his first of three Boston Marathons, he learned that his wife, Jane, had given birth to a son. Cosmas promptly gave him the middle name Boston. Gideon Boston Ndeti.

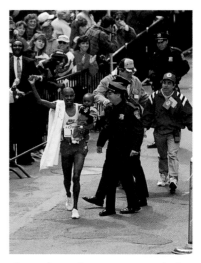

Three-time winner Cosmas Ndeti and son Gideon Boston.

Bill Squires' Simulators

Bill Squires coached Bill Rodgers and the Greater Boston Track Club, the home of the best long-distance runners in the early seventies. Before Squires' innovations, most runners trained by running long distances slowly and then once a week getting on the track to run short distances quickly with very short rest periods. But Squires had his runners running long and quick on the track. They would run fast intervals of 1,600 to 2,400 meters with long rest periods.

Bill Squires.

One special workout Squires conjured up was called a simulator. A simulator was usually conducted at the Boston College track at the 20-mile mark of the Marathon. There the GBTC athletes would run long intervals on the track, then head out running easily to the hills on the Marathon course, which they would run as hard as possible as if in a race, finally returning to the track for more measured timed intervals. This technique and Squires' unique personality are what made the Greater Boston Track Club such a powerhouse.

Tarzan Brown, the Narraganset Indian

Possibly no runner has suffered so much adversity and benefited so little from winning the Boston Marathon as Ellison Myers "Tarzan" Brown. Born poor but with a love and talent for long-distance running, Tarzan Brown won in 1936 and 1939. He tried to use his fame to gain employment. Kelley, Young, Komonen, Pawson, Henigan—all Boston Marathon winners—parlayed their fame into gainful employment. But no one would hire Brown because he was a dark-skinned half–Native American and half-Hispanic man in a predominantly white society.

Brown had an indomitable spirit. When he went with the U.S. Olympic team in 1936 to Hitler's Germany, several Nazi brown shirts accosted him in a Berlin bar. Brown fought back, perhaps thus being the first American to fight the Nazis.

Brown died after a fight outside a barroom, poor and unknown outside the running community, in 1975. Bill Rodgers, who won his first Boston Marathon that year and ushered in a new marathon professionalism, vowed that he did not want to wind up like Tarzan Brown.

Ellison "Tarzan" Brown.

Marathon Marriage

Percy Ellis Morrill of Natick watched the Boston Marathon every Patriots Day of his long life except one—the day he married Mary Davy from Dorchester in 1940.

The Morrill family's history of watching the Marathon goes back to the very first race, when Percy's mother, Agnes Doherety Morrill, walked two miles with her cousins to Natick from South Natick. The family moved to Elm Street in Natick upon her marriage to Percy's father. From that location, one block from the race course, all the cousins gathered yearly to watch the Marathon along with young Percy.

In 1946 Percy and Mary bought a house on West Central Street directly on the race course. Their nine children and 18 grandchildren gather yearly along with 40 cousins to watch the race and have a cookout.

According to Mary Morrill, her husband had some secret code that only the runners understood. She says he seemed to signal them that they could use the bathroom in the house. The runners trotted right in and out again while Percy smiled.

Percy Morrill and Mary Davy.

Uncle John's Respect

Joanne O'Brien has lived in the same house on the
Marathon route all her life. She remembers as a little girl
watching her Uncle John clip the starting roster out of the
newspaper. She could see how much he looked forward to
the race each year.

Watching the race during World War II was depressing.
O'Brien remembers that the number of runners was down
because all the young men had gone off to war (209 men
had started in 1938; only 67 started in 1945). O'Brien
said, "That the runners were respected was the feeling I
had as a child. . . . Respect is what made Kelley a legend,
and that is why the race was heroic and the famous runners
became idols—I learned that from my Uncle John."

Uncle John.

Did you know?

Fire

What could stop the Boston Marathon? Fire. Former Natick Fire Chief Fredette says, "If necessary, we would intercede in the race because public safety comes first." But there is no record of there ever having been a fire in any of the towns along the Marathon route during the race.

The Moleskin Cure

In the burning daylight of the inferno that was the 1976 race, the Natick roads heated to egg-frying temperatures. Still the runners ran. But one runner limped into Ed Ratock's Central Pharmacy. He removed his shoes and asked Ratock, the head pharmacist, if he could help.

Pharmacist Ed Ratock.

Ratock looked at the runner's feet as he peeled a layer of fried skin off the soles of both feet to reveal a tender pinkish-red layer underneath. The runner wanted to continue to Boston, was there anything the pharmacist could do? Ratock grabbed several packages of moleskin off the shelf, then cut and patched pieces over the runner's feet. Off he ran, out the door, no charge, to see if he could make it to Boston.

Two days later, the runner returned to Central Pharmacy to tell Ratock that he had indeed made it to Boston and to thank Ratock for his kind care and attention.

Did you know?

For many years, the myth of the marathon being dangerous to a man's health lingered on. Clarence DeMar liked to tell the story of an old marathon runner who died at age 110. "They say it was the running that killed him."

Wellesley

Wellesley, a wealthy and prestigious suburb of Boston, was first settled in 1630. The settlers paid five pounds in currency and three pounds of corn to Indian chiefs Nehoiden and Mangus for use of the land. Two hundred and fifty years later, the state of Massachusetts incorporated Wellesley on April 6, 1881. It now has a population of over 26,000.

Wellesley College for women was founded in 1875 and now has a student body of 2,300, all of whom seem to line the road in Wellesley to cheer boisterously for the marathoners running past their school.

A Tunnel of Class

Each year Wellesley College students line up along the course in Wellesley and cheer wildly at any excuse. Marathoners call this passage "a tunnel of sound"—in 1992 Ibrahim Hussein, in mock recognition of the din, stuck his fingers in his ears as he ran quickly by. One year they were absent because they were on Easter break, and it was a very quiet Marathon.

In the past, Wellesley students wore long dresses and fur coats as they watched. In modern times, it's jeans and T-shirts. They have given flags and flowers to the leaders. Evidence supporting women's issues generally instigates the greatest volume of Wellesley cheers. For a shirt reading "A year of women on top," the cheers were deafening, as they are also for the woman in the lead and all those who follow her.

The leaders at Wellesley College in 1947.

The Way They Used to Watch

In the early days, long sections of the race course paralleled the railroad tracks. The best seats in the house were in a railway car following the race like a mobile grandstand. Large amounts of money changed hands on those trains. The fans aboard leaned out, screamed at their favorites, and held on to their wallets.

At the same time, everybody who had a bicycle rode along the dirt streets while riders on horseback trotted along to watch. The lead pack was never alone and often shrouded in dust. Later, automobiles had access to the course, and anyone who had a car could ride along the route. For some years, it was pandemonium to Boston.

Wellesley Town Hall.

Spectators.

BOSTON MARATHON: A MIRROR OF HISTORY

The first Boston Marathon started on a dirt road in a quiet country. Few internal combustion engines or electric motors existed. Most people lived and worked on farms. We know our technology is profoundly different; however, the meaning of the marathon foot race has changed just as profoundly. In the past 116 years the Boston Marathon has sharply reflected the changing psychological, economic, and sociological history of Boston, the USA, and the world.

First there was dirt. Dirt and its allotrope, mud, defined the first Boston Marathon course. It had always been so. Three lanes composed roads, one for each wagon wheel and a middle one for the horse. The new wheelmen, or bicyclists, could choose one or the other of the wheel ruts since the hoof prints roughed the middle path. Each runner in the first marathon had a handler on a bicycle follow him to administer aid, much like a handler would attend to a boxer. That collaboration indicates a deeper consideration of what a marathon race meant to the participants and to the public. The marathon was a fight, and you'd better have someone in your corner. That the early marathons would be treated as fights is not surprising, considering that the mythic first marathoner, Pheidippides, was an Athenian foot soldier turned messenger.

Handlers pedaled alongside the runners to administer aid ranging from shots of whiskey to cooling sponges. The use of performance-enhancing devices was allowed. The handler would give a rubdown, unknot cramps, and mostly shout encouragement.

Early newspaper reports told of runners falling to the ground, then rising to run again. They staggered. Reporters referred to the race as "a grind." Runners walked a lot because they were hardly trained, according to current standards. But exhibiting the efficacy of a training program was not the point of the race. Reporters called it "grueling." No one called it fun or enjoyable. The marathon ran as an example and inspiration of young men's courage.

Every schoolboy knew the story of Pheidippides and his exemplary sacrifice. That kind of sacrifice was the thing to do for the world's new nation states. No longer did a young man fight for his tribe or village, but for his country. The marathon symbolized the heroic sacrifice for a cause larger than oneself.

The Boston Marathon did not start small. It was front page news from its very first year with 18 entrants and 10 finishers. People came to watch because they thought someone might die. In the 1900s, notions like Teddy Roosevelt's "The Strenuous Life" took hold. These notions of manliness gripped the world. Men would and should suffer to do the honorable, manly thing and sacrifice themselves for a greater cause. The idea of duty led men to sacrifice themselves on the Titanic in 1912. In 1908 headlines in the US newspapers had read, "Dying Man Wins Marathon." That referred to Dorando Pietri of Italy who didn't win and didn't die in the Olympic Marathon that year in London. He merely almost won and almost died. Pietri entered the Olympic Stadium clearly the leader. He staggered. He fell. He got up. He fell again. Officials helped him across the line. For that he would be disqualified, but as he languished in the hospital, people worldwide waited to see if he would live or die. The public conclusion held that exercise was dangerous and for the very brave or very foolish.

But it was the sense of duty that filled the spirits of the young men who answered the call to fight in

The Boston Marathon did not start small. It was front page news from its very first year with 18 entrants and 10 finishers. People came to watch because they thought someone might die.

WWI. Thousands died while running out of trenches in a futile charge against enemy machine guns. In fact, 1914 Boston Marathon winner, Canadian Jimmy Duffy, died just that brave way a year later in Ypres, France. In 1918, the war canceled the Boston Marathon, replacing it with a "support the troops" military relay race. Then as the world recovered from the "Great War" and learned that it takes more than bravery to win a war, the Boston Marathon saw a subtle change. For the first time, an older man entered the race.

The first master runner in the Boston Marathon was Peter Foley. In 1917, at age 61, he ran 4:11 (24 miles). The officials would not let him race officially because he was too old. By the end of the 1920s many older and better-trained runners raced. This group and its most famous runner, seven-time winner Clarence DeMar, all knew that running was good for a body, but the public did not know that yet. They bet lots of money on their favorites. Numbers of racers rose to 285 starters in 1928. People grew wealthier than ever before as the roaring '20s roared on. But it would not last. The Great Depression in the next decade squashed that growth.

Young men who had once been on farms where the work was endless found themselves in the cities with nothing to do. A small band of volunteers managed the marathon on a shoestring. In the '20s and the Depression years, marathons sent a signal that older men could run a marathon and survive, but oddly the world, while ready for old men, was not ready for women to run. Although Gertrude Ederle swam the English Channel and Amelia Earhart flew solo across the Atlantic, there is no record of any woman wanting to run in the Boston Marathon until 1966. The Boston Athletic Association, founded in 1888 by the movers and shakers of Boston, had been a wealthy, elite organization that had 2,000 members in 1890 and a waiting list. It had a modern clubhouse of gilded-age opulence located at about where the marathon finish line is now. It had a pool inside, a running track, gymnasiums, a billiards room, a fencing salle, a bowling alley, and luxurious amenities for members, including a cigar room. All that fell to pieces during the Depression, as the Boston Athletic Association lost its membership and building. The B.A.A. lost nearly everything. In 1935 the B.A.A. filed for bankruptcy.

The next World War saw the number of racers in the Boston Marathon shrink, but the marathon did go on for every war year. The marathon began to look more and more like a sporting event full of tactics to win and not a death-defying slog. Faster and more athletic men took an interest in the marathon—men who had raced on the track in college. The B.A.A. held on to the marathon and an indoor track meet. A few men, not professionals, held things together.

Leading the charge of fast college runners in the '50s was John J. Kelley. He had represented Boston University on the track and had raced as short as a mile, which he had run in high school in 4:20—an impressive time for a high school runner in the '50s. He won the Boston Marathon in 1957 and is the only member of the B.A.A. to ever do so. At the same time in the fifties, the public attitude toward exercise changed. President Eisenhower played golf. The well-known heart specialist Dr. Paul Dudley White told his patients that exercise is not bad for the heart but good for the heart. People began to see the marathon as an athletic contest and not a struggle to survive the distance. Marathoners themselves began to describe their racing as enjoyable rather than punishment.

During the war years, the number of runners decreased to a low of 67 starters in 1945. Numbers did not increase in the early 1950s beyond the numbers of runners racing the marathon in the 1920s. The volatile and dedicated Scotsman John Duncan Semple managed the B.A.A. and the calmer and just as dedicated Will Cloney managed the race. The race did not need a professional director for the 1960 race with 156 starters. Numbers had not changed for 50 years.

In these post-war years, the country had gone from

isolated regions where young men mostly worked on farms as laborers to a country where ordinary people traveled and resettled more often. Men worked more with machines and their minds. Work and exercise separated. More and more "work" did not require physical exertion. As the country grew smaller, so did the world.

The Boston Marathon attracted Finns, Englishmen, Greeks, Koreans, and Japanese. Much of this attraction to the Boston Marathon came in reaction to the Cold War. The Boston Marathon became another way to show the world that free-market USA was better than communist Russia. In 1963 a pair of Ethopians, Abebe Bikila and Mamo Wolde, came to race the Boston Marathon. They arrived as great favorites, but finished 5th and 12th. Bikila had won the Olympic Marathon in 1960 and would again in 1964 while Wolde would win in Mexico City in 1968. The Boston Marathon became global as the world became global.

Numbers at the Boston Marathon reached 1,000 in 1969. Until then, volunteers operated the marathon by hand. Systems of race management did not exist. Officials took the times by hand, read mechanical stopwatches, and wrote down the finishers' numbers with pencil. The results were then recopied with the runners' names and clubs replacing the numbers. The watches had to be wound to work and on rainy days the officials covered their clipboards with clear plastic bags. To get accurate entries and results for a

1,000 runners was hard. Jock Semple ran race registration out of his training room in the Boston Garden while trying to do his day job. Frequently he lost his

During the war years, the number of runners decreased to a low of 67 starters in 1945.

temper with the interminable phone calls. Clearly, the event had to be controlled.

The first running boom started in the 1970s due to many psychological, economic, and social factors. Great numbers of people, including women, suddenly wanted to race. The race began to appear to people as a celebration of physicality. In the pressure of the Cold War, all the sons (and daughters) of WWII veterans looked to fulfill themselves by doing something very hard. That something was not a military response like the young men of 1916, but nonetheless a powerful urge to be tested. The marathon met that need in a way that service in Vietnam did not. The marathon could be counter culture, but also adherence to the domino theory that US soldiers had to fight communism in Europe so they would not have to fight communists in the US.

The marathon became something of a freedom statement. It stood between the tune in, turn on, and drop out nihilism of the 1960s and 1970s and the straight-arrow military assumption that it is "not mine to reason why, but mine to do or die." Running and training and racing questioned authority but did not ignore discipline and accomplishment. Runners

Running the Boston Marathon has come full-circle to once again be an act of courage.

in the Boston Marathon posted huge numbers of fast times. By the mid 1970s the times for 30th or 50th place would have won almost all Boston Marathons from 1897 into the 1950s.

In the early 1980s, other marathon race organizations recognized the professional potential of the marathon and the revenue stream generated by participants, sponsors, and all the amenities in the cities hosting marathons. So rather than an austere amateur athletic event, the marathon worldwide became a tourist attraction and a profession, but Boston missed the boat. In 1984 and 1985, Boston refused to pay appearance money or prize money to top runners. They went elsewhere, reducing the Boston Marathon to almost a common local road race administered out of a cardboard box.

Out of desperation to save the Boston Marathon, Will

Cloney struck a deal with a clever, opportunist attorney named Marshall Medoff, who obtained the right in perpetuity to "sell" sponsorship of the marathon and keep for himself any amount of money above $400,000. Medoff would own the marathon. The upshot of Cloney's trying to do the right thing for the marathon by raising money, but nearly giving away the race to a private party, caused an uproar in the B.A.A. board. That uproar resulted in Cloney's firing and had nearly lost the marathon. The board engaged Tim Kilduff as volunteer director. He quit after two years in frustration as the rest of the world paid prize money to athletes and Boston would not. The world could not tolerate an amateur marathon run by amateur management. The Boston Marathon itself began to shrink in field quality and newsworthiness, as top runners elected to go elsewhere to compete for a possible payday. The marathon needed professional, full-time management to survive the 1990s.

Without professional management the marathon would have ricocheted from disaster to disaster. John Hancock Financial Services came to the rescue by providing prize money to attract a world-class racing field, space for offices to administer the growing race, and public relations and publicity to attract runners and spectators from around the world to make the Boston Marathon an economic as well as a cultural and athletic force in Massachusetts.

Guy Morse, the first professional director of the Boston Marathon, took control on June 17, 1987. The current director, David McGillivray, has grown with the sport to master all the available technologies of registration, traffic control, volunteer management, results collection, and number pick up.

The B.A.A. has an executive director, club coaching staff, and a professional press relations team. Their offices are fully staffed and efficient. More people now volunteer and work on putting on the marathon than constituted the racing field for most years of its existence. The Boston Marathon is now a big business where once it was a symbol of young men's willingness to sacrifice for country.

The world of marathon racing has gone beyond symbolism and is an opportunity to raise money for charities and causes. More and more people run marathons "for" something or someone. The marathon has come to generate a powerful revenue stream for disease-based charities. This movement may be a reflection of citizens' distrust of government's ability to tax and spend money wisely and a greater willingness to donate to trusted charities that seem to be under the citizen's control.

Now the marathon seems to be reflecting another change in the perception of the event and in the minds of the participants. World Wars and global depressions have influenced the marathon but from a distance. The April 15, 2013, bombing at the finish line of the marathon brought a local urge to defy terrorism. Running the Boston Marathon has come full-circle to once again be an act of courage. The marathon was born in militarism and has returned to it.

Shoes

Nowadays a runner can lace on a pair of shoes out of the box and run to Boston with feet unscathed. It wasn't always so. In the past, more runners were done in by their own shoes than by the weather, the hills, or the tactics of their opponents.

Rosa Mota's shoes and shorts, both size two.

Blisters started with the first Boston Marathon winner, John J. McDermott. By Beacon Street, with miles to go, blisters filled his shoes and the skin began to peel off his feet. This comes as no surprise. McDermott was wearing shoes that were black leather laced to the toe with stiff leather soles stitched to the uppers with waxed thread. The leather itself would shrink or stretch and the soles offered no cushioning. The shoes forced him to walk. Fortunately, he had a gigantic lead. He walked a lot. He said after the race, "This will probably be my last long race. I hate to be called a quitter and a coward, but look at my [bloody] feet."

In 1927 Johnny Miles wanted to defend his title, but he also wanted to break his course record set the year before. His father took his cheap rubber-soled canvas sneakers and carved off all the "excess" rubber. The shoes proved to be light and deadly. Miles didn't make it past seven miles, his feet a mass of bloody blisters.

Oddly enough, blister prevention was aimed at the feet instead of the shoes. Jock Semple took the men he coached to run barefoot in the winter surf on Nahant Beach to toughen their feet.

In the mid-thirties, the coveted shoes were called S.T.A.R. Streamlines. Handmade by a wizard Englishman named Samuel T. A. Ritchins, these shoes indeed were fine. The tops were made of white kidskin with perforations. They laced up the outsides, had tanned calfskin inner liners, a crepe sole, and a metatarsal pad. They weighed 5½ ounces. Each pair took Ritchins 16 hours to make, for which he charged $7.50.

Ted Vogel's shoes.

Bread and Circus

Bread and Circus, a natural foods retailer located across the street from Marathon Sports, does a brisk business on the morning of the Marathon. But like most businesses along the way, they do very little business once the roads close down. The workers go outside and watch the world run by.

Bread and Circus is especially well stocked to help the healthy run by. Employees slice up organic oranges and fill cups with natural spring water and pass out this good sustenance to all runners who need it. There is definitely enough food and drink along the course for any runner who keeps moving to gather a "free" lunch.

Did you know?

Negative Splits

This is the rare occurrence of a runner running the last half of the race faster than the first half. In 1994 Cosmas Ndeti ran the second half of the race in 1:02:15, with a total time of 2:07:15, for the course record. Negative splits are rare, especially at Boston, where the first part of the course is largely downhill. The course record is now 2:03:01.

Patti (Lyons) Catalano

Patti Lyons trained as hard as anyone to win the Boston Marathon. She ran 100 to 140 miles a week in preparation for the 1979 Marathon. She was the favorite that year. But she hadn't always been a runner.

She smoked cigarettes, ate donuts, and drank beer. She was overweight and unhappy before she took up running. But the drive to train paid off. She finished second in 1979 behind Joan Benoit.

In the 1980 race, which Rosie Ruiz spoiled, Patti Lyons was again the favorite, and again placed second behind Jacqueline Gareau. In 1981, Patti (now) Catalano beat Joan Benoit and set an American women's marathon record of 2:27:51, but she once again finished second, this time to Allison Roe of New Zealand.

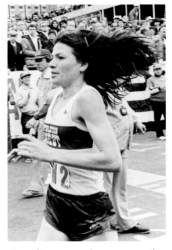

American record setter Patti Catalano in 1981.

Wellesley Runners

JOHN DELANY has lived in Wellesley all his life. He has run the Boston Marathon 10 times. His sister, **NANCY DELANY**, a doctor in the navy, has run five times. On race day John's friends draw a chalk line across the road in Wellesley and place bets predicting when John will cross their line.

PETER STIPE of Wellesley ran his fastest of six races in 1975. He always wore red shorts, and the partisan crowds in Wellesley cheered so loudly for him that his embarrassment turned his face the color of his shorts.

Jimmy Henigan— Unemployed

Jimmy Henigan, Clarence DeMar, Albin Stenroos, and Johnny Miles in 1926.

Jimmy Henigan was the fastest and most talented runner in the Boston area in the twenties and early thirties. He won almost all the cross-country and track races he entered. He had rooms full of trophies, yet without a Boston Marathon victory he felt unfulfilled. Year after year, with great fanfare and press support, he declared that he would win. He ran in the lead or with the leaders, and year after year failed to finish first.

In 1931 Henigan's dream came true: he won the Boston Marathon. His home town of Medford welcomed him with a parade. His photo was in all the newspapers. Everyone shook his hand.

But this was the Depression. By 1933 Jimmy Henigan needed a job to support his large family. The *Boston Post* ran a photo of Henigan on the front page before the race, with a caption asking for a job for the former champion. He ran the race and did not win, but he did find two men waiting for him at the finish line with offers of work.

The B.A.A. vs. the North Medford Club

Jock Semple was quite a good runner in his day, which was 1930. That year he placed seventh in the Marathon. In the forties, fifties, and sixties, coaching the B.A.A. Running Club was his passion. The B.A.A. competed fiercely with the North Medford Club, under Fred Brown Sr. Brown ran in the Boston Marathon many times and appeared to collaborate with Semple in a vociferous feud. The two men secretly liked and admired each other, mostly because they shared the same love of long-distance running and long-distance runners.

Each would go to great lengths to recruit young star runners for their clubs, and each in the process would say the most disgusting things about the other. The last time the North Medford Club won the Boston Marathon team title was in 1972. The B.A.A. came in second. Since then, the team title has gone to other clubs.

Marathon Sports Energy Stop

The Marathon Sports store operated by Colin Petty, an accomplished middle-distance runner, waits for runners to pass by each April. Colin, his wife Penny, and his staff set up an Energy Stop and give away energy food bars and a product called GU™—fast food for athletes—to any runner who needs energy.

One year, a runner stopped in the store during the race because his feet were killing him. Fortunately, he was carrying his credit card. Colin diagnosed the problems the runner had with his old shoes and fitted him properly with a new pair of running shoes, new socks, new singlet . . . in fact, everything he was wearing. Like a race car in a pit stop, the runner left fully repaired to run on.

During the season, Marathon Sports offers a discount to all runners who run to raise money for the Dana-Farber Cancer Institute, in turn donating a portion of those sales.

John J. Kelley— The Great American Hope

The Great American Hope into the early sixties was 1957 winner John J. Kelley, or Kelley the Younger. The previous American to win had been John A. Kelley in 1945 (not related), and the next American winner would be Amby Burfoot in 1968. In between, the press put the burden on John J. Kelley to repel the foreign invaders.

Kelley raced under the mentorship of flamboyant Jock Semple. It was Semple's dream that a B.A.A. runner—wearing the club's emblematic unicorn—would win the B.A.A. Marathon.

Kelley, a Boston University graduate, high school teacher, coach, and writer, held his own philosophy of life and running. He shared his thoughts on nature and life with the young men he coached in a rapid colloquy that took place on the run. Kelley was Henry David Thoreau at six minutes a mile and an inspiration to many Marathon contenders. John J. Kelley died on August 21, 2011.

Kelley and his coach, Jock Semple.

Newton

The area that is now Newton has been attractive to settlers since they first came in the 1630s. The railroad and the mills of Upper Falls and Lower Falls and Nonantum were the area's hot spots, and eventually enough people lived there to elevate Newton to city status in 1873.

Newton now is a town of 83,000 people, and nearly eight miles of the Boston Marathon are run here. Almost all the races are decided in Newton on the hills that separate the winners from the also-rans. More runners drop out in Newton than anywhere else along the course. The favorite dropout place is the tempting Woodland MBTA station, where racers wearing their official numbers are given free fare.

The One and Only Men's World Record

In 1947 Korea was reeling between two wars. That year, Olympic gold medalist Ki Chung Sohn brought the Korean running team to Boston, and his favorite was Yun Bok Suh.

Suh's competition was Finnish champion Mikko Hietanen. As Hietanen and Suh raced shoulder to shoulder through Newton Center, it looked like either could win. Suddenly a fox terrier ran out into the road in front of the Korean runner. Suh tripped over the dog and tumbled to the pavement. The fall scraped his knee and cut his hand. He took a kerchief he carried to wipe away sweat and wrapped it around his bleeding hand. Blood dribbling from his knee as he ran, Suh flew away from the Finn in the Newton hills, went on to win the Boston Marathon, and set a new world's record for men.

From left to right, Mikko Hietanen, Yun Bok Suh, and Ted Vogel in 1947.

Yun Bok Suh gave Korea something to celebrate.

(New standards preclude world records on the Boston course.)

Did you know?

The firehouse in Newton marks the beginning
of the hills.

Ham Radio

The field of play for the Boston Marathon is 26.2 miles, along which are scattered thousands of race workers. How does one end know what the other is doing? Ham radio operators link the 26 Red Cross aid stations operated by 350 volunteers to the race command post in Newton and the medical tent at the finish. They provide information, call for ambulances or police crowd control, and alert specialists about problems coming down the road.

Freedom to Run

Uta Pippig of Germany says, "I have this marathon a little bit in my heart." She grew up in East Germany under the domination of a totalitarian communistic sports administration. They told her when to train, how to train, where to live, where to compete, and what to say.

In 1989 the Berlin Wall fell, and Pippig and her coach/partner Dieter Hogan walked to freedom. Now they could train and race wherever they liked. Boston was one of her first big races. Although she placed second in 1990, the race was a win for her: she gained prize money, endorsement contracts, and a life undreamed of under the old East German dictatorship. She has since won twice. No wonder she finishes every Boston Marathon blowing kisses to the crowd.

Uta Pippig.

BOSTON MARATHON: THE MOVIE
A California director is making a Boston Marathon movie

Southern California native Jon Dunham stood watching the water of the Sudbury River flow over the ancient dam at the site where once stood Metcalf's Mill, in Ashland, Massachusetts. Now the site is called Marathon Park, to commemorate the first start of the Boston Marathon, on April 19th, 1897, when Tom Burke dragged his heel (in some accounts it was his toe) across the dirt road to mark the starting line. Burke, a double Olympic gold medalist sprinter from the first Olympics, a year earlier, shouted "Go!" and made history. Jon Dunham, a filmmaker, is going to make a movie. Many difficulties block his path.

News clips and short films about the Boston Marathon exist. Every year, more news videos are added to the archives, but never has a full-length documentary been made about the Boston Marathon. Jon Dunham wants to make a film about how people of all abilities, different backgrounds, and different motivations go about preparing for a marathon in the year before the race. He wants to tell not just what happened, as in a newsreel, but who wants what and how much they want it.

Boston presents special problems. The film will cost at least $2 million to make. Film crews will be working on marathon day. They will lurk about the course, tracking selected runners whose personal stories will represent the wide swath of emotional reasons people run marathons. The film crew will also document the extensive preparations before the race within meetings of the host B.A.A.'s employees and volunteer

Jon Dunham wants to make a film about how people of all abilities, different backgrounds, and different motivations go about preparing for a marathon in the year before the race.

pool and among the towns and cities disrupted by the marathon race day. For over 100 years, these towns have grown around the marathon course, so unlike new marathons where the course is not designed for current conditions. Security after the bombing of 2013 will be another challenge to document and a large potential danger on marathon day. Police and other security personnel will have to be informed about who is a cameraman and not a gunman and that boxes of filming equipment are just that and not bombs. But Jon Dunham is equipped to understand those complexities. He shot large parts of his last marathon film from moving vehicles in the winding streets of Rome and navigated the winding bureaucracy of Italian municipal officialdom. The movie, *Spirit of the Marathon II*, was released to cinemas in June 2013.

Spirit of the Marathon II captures the journey of seven runners preparing for and running in the Rome marathon. The seven subjects who each ran for unique, but emotionally universal reasons are:

Ylenia, a co-owner of a shoe store in Milan and mother of two;

Julie, from Los Angeles, who picked Rome to be the first of her 52 marathons in 52 weeks to raise money and awareness to fight pancreatic cancer, which claimed her father's life;

Vasyl, a Ukrainian elite runner trying for the last spot on his country's Olympic team;

Epiphanie, a two-time Olympian from Rwanda trying to bring attention to the plight of Rwandan women in her country, which is still recovering from the genocide of 1994;

Scott, whose son died of a drug overdose;

Dominico and Mimmo, who are cousins from Rome.

Dunham and crew intend to find a similar range of people to follow in their preparation, execution, and consequences of Boston 2014.

On race day in Rome, Dunham used a camera crew of 135, a crane, 16 golf carts, and two helicopters. Golf carts cannot be allowed on the Boston course, so other cinematographic techniques will have to be used.

The film about the Boston Marathon will be similar but different in the ways individual personalities, motivations, and talents differ and because cities and times differ. Each of the towns along the course is a character with its own history and motivation. The host, B.A.A., will be a character in the movie too. It has a long, wrinkled, and sometimes curmudgeonly personality. Training in Boston has its annoying problems. Storms can ruin the best plans. Training on ice is tricky. Some winter days in Boston blow so cold that experienced men run wearing three socks—only two of them on their feet. But Boston is not Rome. Boston is also not Chicago. Boston is not New York. The 2012 NYC marathon could not be run because of Super Storm Sandy. Boston has not been canceled by a storm, yet. The Massachusetts Department of Public Safety could order the race not to be held for safety or security reasons and there would be nothing the

B.A.A. or a mere filmmaker could do about it.

Dunham began making films at age 13. From then he chose filmmaking as a career and has pushed singularly forward with that relentless mindset of a marathon racer—but he wasn't a marathoner yet.

In a meet-the-filmmakers interview with Thomas White, Dunham said:

"I grew up around photography. My father lived in the Yosemite Valley when Ansel Adams had a studio there, so as far back as I can remember there were these remarkable black and white landscapes of monuments like Half Dome, El Capitan, Yosemite Falls, all around the house. This created a lasting impression on me, and I love nature and photography to this day.

"I began making films when I was 13 years old, using my family's Hi8 camcorder. Through video, I completely fell in love with motion pictures, and it wasn't long before I was 'documenting' everything I could think of. I married the formal quality of the photographs I had known growing up with my growing interest in people and real life stories, and I found my way into the world of nonfiction film."

He graduated in 2000 from the University of Southern California's School of Cinematic Arts. Top Value Television pioneer Megan Williams chose him as the cinematographer for *Tell Me Cuba*, a documentary about the difficult and complex relations between the United States and Cuba. The collaboration continued with Dunham's directorial debut, *No Distance Too Far*, a documentary featuring four individuals, whose lives had been touched by AIDS, as they took part in the California AIDS Ride, which involved 3,000 cyclists on nearly 600 miles of California coast. The film shows how over the course of the ride they grieve for lost friends and family members and worry about the expanding pandemic as they embrace life and support each other. The film was featured in the International Documentary Association's 2002 Doctober Festival of Outstanding Films.

Filming his next journey took five years, as he teamed with Academy Award winner Mark Jonthan Harris, who would executive produce the shooting and directing of the first *Spirit of the Marathon* in Chicago.

As a teenager in Los Angeles, Dunham knew about running only from television. His school had no track team or cross-country team. He had watched the L.A. marathon on the small screen. One day when he was 15, he saw L.A. marathon entry blanks on the counter of a Subway sandwich shop. How hard could it be? He filled out the form and sent it in. On race day he needed a ride from his parents to the start. Since it was L.A. in 1993, they along with thousands of others got stuck in a massive traffic jam. Start time approached. Dunham saw runners jump out of their cars to run to the start. So he jumped out too. His mother thought she would never see him again as he joined the panicking runners weaving through the stalled traffic to the exit ramp.

He made it to his jammed corral in time for the gun. For the first mile he thought the pace was easy. No problem. I can run forever like this, he thought. But by the halfway turn-around in Hollywood, he found himself walking. He didn't know how he would get back to the start. It is funny to think of the future filmmaker stuck in Hollywood. He reached the finish in 5:06:59. But the day transformed him. After great pain and a long pensive time to think about the difficulty of each subsequent step, the finish line loomed into sight. Why do people do this? He wondered. Why did I decide to do this? He crossed the line. That moment, that relief, formed him and pushed him to capture that feeling of accomplishment, release, fulfillment, and resolve to improve, to fill the unforgiving minute (or hours) with distance running. He knew why he ran. He wanted to tell everyone else. He wanted them to feel that feeling. He wants to memorialize that combination of joy and relief in a film:

"I try not to sound too evangelical about running because I know it's not for everyone, but my hope is that people will see this and even if running doesn't take with them, something else will. They'll get out and rediscover the bicycle or swimming or tennis or whatever it may be. To be active. I'm passionate about being physically active in whatever form that takes. I think it really makes life more enjoyable."

About his first marathon film he says:

"*Spirit of the Marathon* is a very personal film to me. That first marathon changed my life. It was by far the most difficult thing I had ever experienced. I've run at a minimum one marathon a year since then and the energy, spectacle, diversity, and camaraderie

He knew why he ran. He wanted to tell everyone else. He wanted them to feel that feeling.

around the event continues to inspire me. I had to capture at least a small part of the significance of the marathon in my life."

He improved his marathon time to 3:22:39 in Chicago in 2001.

"Furthermore, I credit the marathon with instilling in me a sense of empowerment that has had a profound influence on the rest of my life, not the least of which being my decision to pursue a career in film. In this way, running my first marathon is very much related to the deep, inner resources that I've had to discover and use in my own filmmaking," Dunham said.

When Dunham came from Southern California to Ashland and Hopkinton and toured the Boston course on a pleasant summer day, the greenness and lush beauty of the towns and neighborhoods along the course impressed him. Lawns and flowers and bright green shrubbery refreshed him in contrast to the tan and muted green of California hills. Dunham began to think of how to capture all that vivid color until his tour guide reminded him that Boston in April is not Boston in August. Trees in April have no leaves. If the sun shines, stark shadows of branches fall across the road. If the sun does not shine, the predominate color is gray. April is the cruelest month. The cinematographer may shoot in color but he will get black and white. Sometimes rain falls hard. A north-

Making a film about the Boston Marathon will be more of a challenge than running it.

east storm could blow off the ocean. Sometimes the weather runs through all these changes during the race. It has snowed. Temperatures have sometimes been slightly above freezing in a driving rain—not good for film crews or equipment. Making a film about the Boston Marathon will be more of a challenge than running it.

Special legal agreements will have to be made in the year after the Boston Marathon bombing. It has paid off in the marathon/movie business for Dunham twice already, but as they say in advertisements about investments, "Past performance is no guarantee of future performance."

In many ways, making a movie about a marathon is a marathon and full of vicissitudes—heartbreaks and disappointment of the sport. You may never get to the starting line because of injury in preparation—a movie maker could run out of money, or breakdowns in personnel or equipment could produce a film that is not what was hoped for, or maybe after everything goes well, cinemas may not want it. Dunham is committed to making this movie and, like marathoners, he will do whatever it takes to reach the finish line.

Not only will the film company that Dunham and his producer, Megan Williams, lead face weather, they will also have to deal with strict limits imposed by security. Each town on the course has its own police force and is responsible for enforcing safety. Each police chief will have to think that his or her community might be the target of terrorists. Their policies may differ, but Williams has experience in dealing with the vagaries of movie making. She is the recipient of numerous awards, including an Academy Award Nomination and the Alfred I. duPont—Columbia University School of Journalism Award. In 2002, she teamed with Dunham on *No Distance Too Far*. Her work covers a variety of topics and events including: the Democratic and Republican Conventions, the Super Bowl, the Oscars, Bob Dylan's Hard Rain Concerts, HIV/AIDS, and childhood deafness.

From 1996 to 2000, Williams served as adjunct professor at the University of Southern California's School of Cinema-Television. Her work in the 1970s as cofounder and partner of TVTV—one of the first independent documentary video organizations—is featured in Diedre Boyle's *Subject to Change: Guerrilla Television Revisited* (Oxford University Press, 1997). Dunham is committed to make the film. He is a filmmaker. Just as marathoners come to Boston in defiance of danger and the hardness of the event, Dunham and company will make a film about the Boston Marathon one way or another. Every gram of endurance Dunham and company can muster will go to bringing the Boston Marathon Movie to a theater near you.

The Day Billy Saved Alberto

Back in the mid-1970s, when Bill Rodgers was the top runner in the Greater Boston Track Club, high school runner Alberto Salazar tagged along on the team runs. Salazar would one day run faster than Rodgers, winning the 1982 Boston Marathon, but as a teenager he had trouble keeping up. They nicknamed Salazar the "Rookie."

One day, Rodgers, who ran in a detached way looking all around, noticed Salazar being attacked by a very large dog. Salazar had dropped off the pace, and the other runners had not noticed and kept going. The Great Dane had bowled the teenager over into a ditch and was snarling at him eye to eye. Salazar expected to be eaten. Rodgers, no giant himself, ran back and chased the dog away by throwing his car keys at the monster.

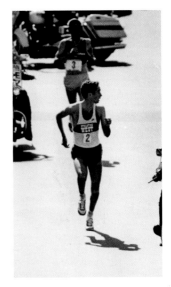

Dick Beardsley pushed Alberto Salazar (No. 2) to the limit in 1982.

How Heartbreak Hill Got Its Name

In 1936 Johnny A. Kelley was the defending champion, a runner who wore his heart on his sleeve and desperately wanted to win again. But he had not counted on the talents of Narraganset Indian Ellison Myers "Tarzan" Brown.

Brown was frequently unable to control his quickness. He would zip out to large leads early in races only to have lack of conditioning reduce him to a walk. This year, Brown zipped and Kelley waited. On the top of the last hill in Newton, Kelley caught Brown. Assuming he would trot on to victory, Kelley gave Brown a pat on the behind and took the lead. This gesture galvanized Brown. He caught up to Kelley and ran away to victory. *Boston Globe* reporter Jerry Nason named that last Newton hill "Heartbreak" and the name stuck.

Andres Espinoza (No. 4) leads in his course-record charge over Heartbreak Hill in 1994.

Amby Burfoot

Amby Burfoot was an 18-year-old college freshman at Wesleyan when he ran his first Boston Marathon in 1965. A runner used to running two-mile races in high school, he saw the small bright orange sign reading "19 7/8 miles to go," and thought it absurd. But having committed himself to the race, he kept running. He finished an effortless race—a feeling he never again experienced in a marathon. But it was too late: he was hooked.

Three years later, in 1968, with great effort and trepidation that he would be passed at any moment by a superior runner he had never seen, or get a cramp, or slow down—but with the same feeling of awe and incredulity—he won.

Amby Burfoot.

Did you know?

Course Elevations

The course starts at 490 feet above sea level, drops to 60 feet in Newton Lower Falls where it crosses the Charles River, rises to 230 feet at the top of Heartbreak Hill, and descends to the finish 10 feet above sea level.

Newton Town Hall.

Johnny Miles: An Unlikely Winner

Johnny Miles won the Boston Marathon in 1926 and in 1929. Miles grew up on Cape Breton in Nova Scotia where as a youth he worked in the mines during the war.

As a curly haired, freckle-faced kid, Miles came to Boston in 1926 intending to win. He wore a pair of 98-cent sneakers and faced Olympic champion Albin Stenroos and the already-legendary Clarence H. DeMar. Miles worshipped Stenroos, but on the yet-to-be-named Heartbreak Hill, Miles somewhat tentatively passed his idol. When Stenroos did not respond, the young Miles ran away to victory.

Johnny Miles in 1926.

Miles became the toast of Boston. The Boston Post's front page read, "Unknown Kid Smashes Record." Miles came back to Boston in 1927, but blisters forced him out of the race. With his blood-filled shoes and sweaty body, he took a ride to the finish and faced the jeers of the press. "The loser who walks off the field is some part of a thief," wrote one reporter.

Miles came back and won again in 1929. He ran in two Olympic marathons. He passed away in 2003 at the age of 97.

Newton Runners

BOB CLIFFORD has run the Boston Marathon 19 times. In 1983 he was living with four others in an apartment directly on the course. When he ran by, he was shocked to see a big party raging in his apartment. He was tempted to crash the party, which seemed to be in his honor, but dropping in would spoil it, so he ran on.

HUBERT JESSUP, who moved to the Boston area in 1968 to be general manager of Boston Neighborhood network TV, watched the Marathon for years before he began running it in 1991. He has run every year since. He said, "At last I got around to running it myself after I had been so impressed by the power of the community celebration surrounding it; now I'll always run it. It is the goal and focus of my athletic year."

Causes and Charities

The winners run for glory and prize money. Others run to set personal records or to finish as high as possible in the final standings. But some run for causes larger than themselves.

The Massachusetts Association of the Blind (MAB) sponsors a team of runners without vision problems to run the Marathon with the visually impaired. In 2013 they raised more than $78,000. More than 300 runners run to raise money for the Dana-Farber Cancer Institute. They are coached by 1976 Marathon winner Jack Fultz. Each member of the Leukemia and Lymphoma Society Team in Training runs the race in honor of patients battling illnesses, raising money through pledges. A Run for Research team raises money for the American Liver Foundation. Other charity teams benefit the Muscular Dystrophy Association and the National Spinal Cord Injury Association. The 1984 and 1985 winner, Geoff Smith, launched his own charity effort to benefit the Shriners Burns Institute and the Ron Burton Training Village.

Some runners run for glory, others carry a pledge sheet.

Quincy police Charles Santoro, Joseph Murphy, and Steven O'Brien.

Adam Walsh and the American Liver Foundation

Adam Walsh of Boston had no intention of running the Marathon. He had run cross-country in high school, but as a full-time medical student he only ran on weekends. When his father was diagnosed with terminal liver cancer, Walsh was devastated. His father was in great pain, and Adam felt helpless. Then a childhood friend told him about the American Liver Foundation and the Boston Marathon.

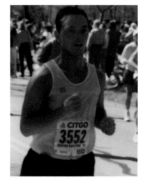

Adam Walsh in 1995.

The American Liver Foundation arranges with the Boston Marathon for fund-raising runners to be exempt from the usual strict entry requirements. Adam signed up. Although he knew his fund raising would not help his father, he felt that he was doing something that might help others.

The outpouring of letters and responses from family and friends astonished Walsh. He raised $8,000 for the Liver Foundation and ran a decent 3:48 marathon. At mile 16, his spirits lifted when a longtime friend cheered him on with a sign reading, "Run for Research, Go Adam."

For Kids Only

Children under age 18 are not allowed to run in the Marathon. So the day before the Marathon, the Newton Heartbreak Hill International Youth Race is run up and down Heartbreak Hill in Newton.

The race is a mile long and starts between Newton City Hall and the Kelley statue. There are 20 starts for boys and girls in divisions grouped by age. The prizes are seedling trees. In 2011, 300 children ran in the race. "It would be wonderful to see one of these kids grow up to win the big Marathon someday," said Stanley Gaffin of the Newton Pride Committee, which sponsors the race.

The boys' start in 1995.

Did you know?

World Records Set at Boston

1947, Yun Bok Suh, Korea, 2:25:39

1975, Liane Winter, West Germany, 2:42:24

1983, Joan Benoit, USA, 2:22:43

THE BOSTON MARATHON

61 Boston Marathons

Born in 1907, John A. Kelley ran 61 Boston Marathons between 1928 and 1992. He watched his first Boston Marathon in 1921 and remembered how effortlessly the plumber from New Jersey, Frank Zuna, ran past to win. Kelley was 20 years old when he started his first race—although he did not finish it—and 84 when he started his last, which took him five hours and 58 minutes. He ran his fastest time at age 37 in 1943 in a race where he placed second to the effervescent Quebecois Gerard Cote.

John A. Kelley.

As a 10-year-old boy, Kelley wanted to be a champion baseball player, but he didn't have the eye for it. He did, how-ever, have the courage. When told that the secret to hitting the ball is to stand still, keep your eye on the ball, and wait for it to come to you, Kelley did just that. He did not move until the ball hit him in the eye. Kelley took this unflinching stick-to-itiveness to the sport of running.

Kelley said he looked forward to aging and that life began at 40. He had won the Boston Marathon in 1935 and remarkably again 10 years later in 1945. He felt the heartbreak of second place seven times. No one has come close to Kelley in the number of Boston Marathons run. Said Kelley, "Running is a way of life for me, just like brushing my teeth. If I don't run for a few days, I feel as if something's been stolen." Kelley died on October 6, 2004.

Young at Heart: this statue of young man Kelley of 1935 and old man Kelley of the nineties stands on Heartbreak Hill in Newton.

DON'T EVEN TRY TO SET A WORLD RECORD AT BOSTON

Regardless of how fast you run on the Boston Marathon course, you cannot set a world record. Ever. It is against the rules to set a world record on the Boston Marathon course. The Boston Marathon has been around since 1897, so you would think it might know the rules and would conform to them. The B.A.A., which manages the marathon, knows the rules full well but defies them for good reason. You might think that the defiance is a stubborn Boston thing, but there is more to the story.

First there is the rule. Bostonians don't like rules, but sometimes rules are a good thing. Here are two portions of rule 265 in the 2013 International Athletics Federation rule book:

For all road records:

(a) The course must not have a net decrease in elevation from start to finish exceeding 1 part per thousand (i.e., 1m per km).

(b) The start and finish of the race must lay no more than 50 percent of the race distance apart as measured along the straight line between them.

(c) The course must be verified (i.e. re-measured)

as late as possible before the race, on the day of the race or as soon as possible after the race, in accordance with Rule 240.3.

2013 USATF Competition Rules • 158

The Boston course conforms to all those rules. Nevertheless, it is point to point and downhill. The distance is accurate—measured by the book—but the course will not conform to an attempt to tame it by binding it to approximate a running track. The course is almost a straight line, not anything like an oval. From the start to the finish in a perfect straight line, regardless of roads, the distance is 24 miles, so it curves very little. This means that the wind can blow at the runners' backs aiding them throughout the race. The course loses 495 feet from start to finish or 3.3 meters per kilometer, clearly in violation of rule 265. The Boston Marathon course does not comply with the rules meant to standardize marathon courses throughout the world so times could be compared and records set like on a track.

It is good marketing to be able to promote a marathon course as having the potential for a world record. Then the race can invite the world record holder or almost world record holders and provide the means to deliver great advertising value to their sponsors.

The downhills take a toll on a runner's thighs, and all the little rolling hills through Wellesley and Natick bang bones and muscles into each other. On a day with a slow, warm, following wind, runners easily overheat, because the wind approximates their running speed giving them little help, but prevents their own sweat from evaporating. On some days in April, Boston temperatures have reached over 100°F, and on other days, rain slightly above freezing has fallen. A loop course would even these extremes with a change in wind direction. Times from year to year would not be so radically different. But standardization is not why Bostonians founded their marathon.

Boston will not change the course of the marathon to make it more uniform like a track. One could design a loop course that starts and ends in the city. It could

It is against the rules to set a world record on the Boston Marathon course.

follow Paul Revere's ride, but those roads barely exist. An out-and-back course would conform to the rule. In Boston, the prevailing winds blow from the west, so more often the race has a tailwind. Geoffrey Mutai ran 2:03:02 in 2011—faster than a marathon had ever

been run. The wind blew him to Boston at 15 to 20 mph. Four men broke 2:05. For two years afterwards, no one broke 2:10. The winds of change in the marathon world, however, brought a need to be able to sanction and certify a world record. Boston listens to a longer tradition than most marathons because it is older, stubborn, and has its own story to tell.

The Olympic marathon is older than the Boston Marathon. It started on the plains of Marathon and ran to Athens in 1896 to commemorate the mythic run of Pheidippides who had come from a long way away to announce victory. He did not run in a circle, so subsequent Olympic marathons ran from starts far away from the Olympic stadium where crowds waited as if they were waiting for the news on the marathon battle. That is the original symbolism—a messenger is coming. In subsequent Olympiads the marathon course became a celebration of the city at the end of the contested games where the spectators waited in the stadium for news.

In 1900 the Olympic marathon started in the stadium in Paris and looped the Seine and the city. The course put Paris on display as much as the competing athletes. The Olympic Marathon in 1904 ran on a hot, dusty loop in St. Louis; that was not Paris or anything remotely like civilized Paris. It was America just west of the Mississippi, raw and wild. He had everyone fooled for a few minutes. In 1908, it again ran point to point in London, starting at the

Windsor Castle and continuing for a distance of 26 miles and 385 yards, instead of about 24 miles as it had been. Later that exact distance became the standard—some people say because the royal family wanted to watch the start from their castle, which proved to be the first of many decisions to standardize and civilize the marathon. The Boston Marathon, however, was already a decade old.

Each Olympic Marathon is unique and tries to be so. In the 1960 Rome Olympic Games, the marathon event, born in the glory of ancient Greece, ran past the grand symbols of the Roman Empire at night down torch-lit streets from the start at the most

Boston listens to a longer tradition than most marathons because it is older, stubborn, and has its own story to tell.

sacred of the seven Roman Hills, Campidoglio with a plaza designed by Michelangleo, past the statue of Marcus Aurelius, along the Appian Way, to finish at Arch of Constantine built in 315 AD next to the Colosseum. Abebe Bikila won running barefoot. Each marathon requires different tactics, respecting the contours and the weather, as well as the competition. In a marathon, course is character,

but not so with tracks. Tracks are meant to be manufactured clones of each other, but marathon courses have the personalities of the places they pass. The magic of the marathon is that it harkens to an untamed era, but the magic of the track is standardization. The track is tamed, but the marathon reminds us of our wild nature. The value is in the difference. The Boston Marathon insists on keeping that wildness—even the name refuses to be tamed. The name of the Boston Marathon is inaccurate if you think of the marathon as being in Boston. It is really a race outside of Boston that is run mostly in other towns and cities en route to the goal destination.

The marathon reeks of symbolism and history—deep history. As their first "sport," humans fought each other, and track and field—the basis of the Olympic Games—reminds us of war in a stadium—with the throwing of spears and cannon balls and the leaping over barriers in a charge to victory against an enemy camp. Track and field is engineered and civilized to produce results as a measure of human performance against an absolute standard—a world record. But the marathon since its origins has meant more than a footrace that is held to measure human performance; it is a symbol as well as a footrace. The marathon is outside the stadium and outside the limits of engineered sport comparing athlete to a standard rather than a competitor. The marathon stands for something ultimate so it is held on the last day of the Olympic Games, run from some great distance to bring a message to the waiting crowd in the stadium. The marathon reminds us that there have always been soldiers who made the ultimate sacrifice for country. It is not an accident or convenience that the Boston Marathon is held on Patriots Day. The marathon is a memorial that symbolizes effort against geography, the limits of breath and the heart, to declare final victory over great pain. The marathon is four times longer than the next longest Olympic running race. It was never meant to be like the rest of track and field. The marathon is more than a measure of physical athletic prowess. It takes a psychological measure. The marathon stands in contrast to a cool world of precise scientific measurement of muscle against millimeters. Time is not the only thing to measure in a race, because if it were, ever more silly things would happen in pursuit of fast times.

A marathon in Utah called the Big Cottonwood Marathon starts up a canyon at about 9,800 feet and finishes at about 4,200 feet. That is about a mile drop or about 10 times the Boston drop. Felix Baumgartner, the Austrian skydiver, took a balloon up to the edge of space and jumped off. He set a world record for the highest vertical velocity, but it was not a marathon because he was only 24 miles high. It took him less than 10 minutes, as he

reached 834 miles per hour. Of course trying to make a marathon course as fast as possible will lead to silliness, but long before that, making the course easier subverts the symbolism and tradition of the marathon. That is why the B.A.A. is unlikely to change the course to be faster, slower, more convenient, or in compliance with the rules. Boston is older than the rules, and if no one can ever set a world record on the course, well, winning should be good enough.

We may have the technology soon to measure the genetic potential of a human athlete and combine that with a scientific protocol of nutrition and a training program. We might be able to change the road surface to be perfectly compliant with optimal human performance, as are some fast indoor tracks— a perfect degree of bounciness. We could plan for the wind and the angle of the sunlight. We could employ pacers by the kilometer. We could construct marathon courses so each matches the other as closely as our technology allows. But then the wildness would be gone. Gone would be the respect for the courageous Greek warrior, Pheidippides, who ran over the wild hills of Greece to declare, "Rejoice, we are victorious," then died.

Boston in
BRIGHTON

Only a tiny portion of the Marathon course passes through the Brighton neighborhood of Boston. It is a densely populated residential area packed with apartments. When the race reaches Brighton, it is definitely in the city. The crowd thickens as the race route begins to parallel the Green Line Trolley. The trolley, with its horizontal green stripe, often keeps pace with the runners, giving the riders the luxury of a mobile grandstand view. But the Marathon route stays in Brighton for less than a mile before it plunges into Cleveland Circle from Lake Street and runs on into Brookline.

Cleveland Circle . . .

. . . where there is no circle. When Japanese runners came to tour the course, they were shown Cleveland Circle. They looked around for a circle. There isn't one.

What was in the "Circle" was the Bill Rodgers Running Center, which had become a beacon attracting runners from all over. Many top runners supported themselves by selling shoes and giving running advice. The store had a shower, and any runner in serious training was welcome to stop by, pick up a training partner, run out to the Newton hills and back, shower, and hang around. So there was a circle of marathon runners regularly orbiting Bill Rodgers' store.

Another tangled place-name is Coolidge Corner. Those unfamiliar with the course might expect the route to turn a corner here, but it doesn't.

There is no circle at Cleveland Circle.

Greg Meyer:
The Last American

Boston in the late seventies was the running capital of the world. Greg Meyer came to train with the Greater Boston Track Club and all the fabulous runners that club had attracted. Frequently Alberto Salazar, winner in 1982, four-time winner Bill Rodgers, and two-time Olympian Pete Pfitzinger would run world-class workouts with half a dozen other members.

Meyer worked in Bill Rodgers' store in Cleveland Circle between his twice-daily workouts. There always was some-one to train with. As of this writing, he was the last American to win the Boston Marathon.

Greg Meyer in 1983.

Race Directors

The race director commands all the amenities and support of a major corporate CEO. But it wasn't always so for the man in charge of the Marathon. At one time it operated out of a cardboard box in B.A.A. Running Club coach and manager Jock Semple's trainer's room in the old Boston Garden. A gruff and bellicose Scotsman, John Duncan "Jock" Semple worked for the Celtics, but his true love was the Boston Marathon and marathon runners.

Management of the Marathon was a labor of love. Semple and director Will Cloney, who managed the race through the fifties, sixties, and into the boom years of the seventies, worked at other full-time jobs. They held their beloved Marathon together on a shoestring budget.

Now the Marathon alone is bigger than John Graham, the director in 1897, could have dreamed. But Graham and his cohorts would not be surprised to see the B.A.A., more than one hundred years later, operating the biggest sporting event in Boston's history.

Former marathon director Guy Morse.

Jock Semple.

The First Wheelchair Racer

Bob Hall, a member of the Greater Boston Track Club, had competed in shorter races in a wheelchair. In 1975 he asked B.A.A. officials if he could join the race, and they agreed. Furthermore, if he broke three hours, he would get an official finishing certificate. He finished the race in 2:58.

Bob Hall, the first wheelchair racer, in 1975.

By 1995 Bob Hall had become the father of wheelchair racing and the world expert in the design and manufacture of racing wheelchairs. He again competed in the Marathon in a wheelchair of his most recent design, and he finished 33rd with a time of 1:47:41. Part of his improved finish time was the result of technical improvements in wheelchair design. But mostly it was due to what wheelchair racers had learned about training and racing techniques in 20 years. Hall at age 44 was a tougher and better-trained competitor.

The wheelchair division of the Boston Marathon is now limited to experienced racers who have met strict qualifying standards. The Boston Marathon has become the world championship for wheelchair racers.

Racing wheelchairs now use the ultimate in high technology.

Never on a Sunday?

Why run the race on a Monday when the rest of the country goes to work? Wouldn't it be better if the race were run on a Sunday, and it could be televised during the usual sports programming hours? Tradition dictates that the Boston Marathon be held on Patriots Day, and Patriots Day now falls on the third Monday in April.

The race was moved to Sunday twice during World War II at the request of Governor Saltonstall. Because of the war effort, Patriots Day was a workday, and he wanted defense workers to be able to watch.

In previous years, before many U.S. holidays were moved to Mondays, if April 19 fell on a Sunday, the race would be held on Saturday or Monday instead.

Patriots Day commemorates the midnight ride of Paul Revere and the other riders who spread the alarm that the Redcoats were marching on the munitions stored in Lexington and Concord. Thus began the war that separated the colonies from Great Britain and gave birth to the United States of America.

One reason the Boston Marathon has endured for a whole century is the interlocking symbolism of the American Revolution, the struggle of men and women athletes to attain a distant goal, and the celebration of spring at the end of another miserable New England winter.

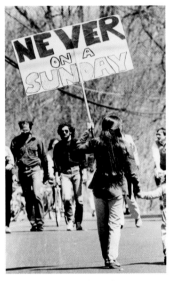

Protesters marched in 1982 when officials discussed changing Marathon day to Sunday.

Did you know?

Course Records

Men's open: Geoffrey Mutai, Kenya, 2:03:02 in 2011

Women's open: Margaret Okayo, Kenya, 2:20:43 in 2002

Men's masters: John Campbell, New Zealand, 2:11:04 in 1990

Women's masters: Firia Sultanova-Zhdanova, Russia, 2:27:58 in 2002

Men's wheelchair: Joshua Cassidy, Canada, 1:18:25 in 2012

Women's wheelchair: Wakado Tsuchida, Japan, 1:34:06 in 2011

John Campbell.

Brookline

Brookline is the smallest town on the route, only 6.7 square miles but jammed with 59,000 people. In quieter times, the 1830s, Brookline was sought by prosperous Boston merchants as a place for country homes and refuge from the clatter of horse hooves and steel-rimmed wagon wheels on the commercial cobblestone streets of Boston.

In one small piece of Brookline history, the 35th president of the United States, John Fitzgerald Kennedy, was born here at 83 Beals Street in 1917.

On Marathon day, all along Beacon Street, the crowds cluster on the rooftops and balconies of stylish apartments, partying and spectating with banners and beer, cheering the runners through.

Joan Benoit Goes Red Sox

Boston College.

Joan Benoit expected to take the lead sometime during the Boston Marathon of 1979, but she knew that was not enough. Once taken, the lead must be kept. She remembered how often her heart had been broken by her favorite baseball team, the Boston Red Sox. Early in the season, the team often showed great promise to win the pennant and the World Series. They often led the league by an astounding margin only to blow it.

Joan wanted to be reminded not to blow her lead, so she had a friend wait for her along the course to hand her a Red Sox baseball cap. Baseball fans along the remaining miles cheered for her hat. And with the cap on her head, she won the World Series of running.

Greece on His Shirt

Stylianos Kyriakides came to Boston in 1946 to run and win in the name of the Greek people who were suffering terrible food shortages following World War II. The Nazis had devastated Greece in their violent and merciless occupation during the war, and the country reeled in desperate need of aid. The only country intact after the war was the victorious United States. Kyriakides, with the support of his people, who kept him fed while he trained despite the shortages, wanted to win so that he could use the publicity to get help for his country.

Kyriakides had run in Boston before the war. When he returned in 1946, he was a leaner, harder man. Kyriakides beat Johnny A. Kelley, the local favorite, and the people of Greece received the food aid they so badly needed.

Stylianos Kyriakides.

Politicians Run Too

As a young man in 1946, Mike Dukakis thrilled with the rest of Boston's Greek community to see Stylianos Kyriakides win the race and make his plea for help for the people of Greece.

In 1951 Dukakis ran the Boston Marathon himself in a decent 3:31 for 57th place. He ran with a high school friend, Reed Wiseman, and both set out at 6:50 per mile. Soon that pace became difficult, and Dukakis fell back with cramps, but they cleared up with two miles to go and he finished strong.

Then in 1988, as governor of Massachusetts, Dukakis ran for president of the United States.

Mike Dukakis.

A River Runs Through It

The Boston Marathon is a significant event for the towns it runs through. The quiet of the suburban area is broken by an influx of runners and spectators that briefly consumes each town. All along the route, the runners flow into town like a flood-swollen river breaching its banks.

For hours, the residents cannot move north or south across the route. Even emergency vehicles are sometimes barred from passing, so the towns post fire trucks, ambulances, and police on both sides of the route. Thousands of police officers direct traffic and control the crowds.

Each town's department of public works makes sure that the Marathon roads are the first to be repaired from the winter's damage. The citizens of the towns also often clean up the litter left on public and private property. But despite all the inconvenience, the townspeople eagerly line the road and cheer. It is their town and their Marathon race, and they are proud of both.

The flood of runners.

Ambulances getting ready.

Prerace Pasta Party

The prerace pasta party is a carbohydrate carnival. On two levels of the Boston World Trade Center, runners from all parts of the world meet and exchange T-shirts, pins, badges, stories, names, and addresses. They network despite nervousness while fueling up for the coming race.

Guido Genicco and Cesarina Taroni at the pasta party in 1990.

New friends make plans to find each other on the race course and run together. Instant bonds form that often last for years. Runners meet and plan to meet again. "Same time next year?" "No, faster." Perhaps a few romances will kindle.

In 1995 the party fell on Passover and Easter, so an Easter bunny roamed around the hall, and matzo balls were also served. Jugglers and face painting entertain the kids. A flotilla of navy ships ties up on the nearby docks for tours. Yet, fun as it all is, the party ends early, because everyone has miles to go after they sleep.

Did you know?

Pasta Party Menu

5,800 pounds of pasta

2,000 quarts of tomato sauce

5,200 cloves of garlic

20,000 rolls

400 pounds of salad

2,160 containers of parmesan cheese

16,000 ice cream bars

20,000 cookies

BROOKLINE

Postrace Party

Unlike the pasta party, the party after the race rolls till all hours. It is raucous and filled with the worst dancers ever. The runners, gleeful but stiff from racing, try to dance but do so with little grace. They wear their T-shirts and medals proudly. They talk over the music as the tension of the training and the race explodes into incessant conversation. Romances that budded in the prerace party now bloom. Runners watch the race highlights on big-screen video and wind down joyously.

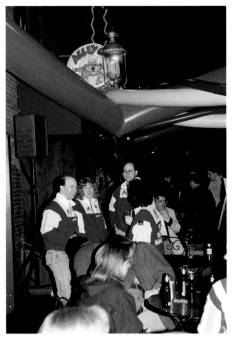

Runners celebrate at a postrace party at the Alley Cat.

Did you know?

The Connecticut Connection

John J. Kelley, the 1957 winner, taught and coached Groton, Connecticut, high school student Amby Burfoot, who won the 1968 race. Amby Burfoot roomed at Wesleyan College (in Connecticut) with Bill Rodgers, who won the race in 1975, 1978, 1979, and 1980. Bill Rodgers invited Greg Meyer to come to Boston to live and train, and Greg Meyer won the race a few years later, in 1983.

Coolidge Corner.

THE BOSTON MARATHON

A Phalanx of Motorcycles

In 1980 President Jimmy Carter ordered the U.S. boycott of the Olympic Games in Moscow after the Soviet invasion of Afghanistan. Bill Rodgers protested. He was likely to be a member of the Olympic team, and he wanted to go.

Rodgers' controversial position against the president elicited death threats. Someone called the Bill Rodgers Running Center to say that Rodgers would never make it to Coolidge Corner alive. To protect him, police motorcycles formed a phalanx around Rodgers.

The police kept him safe. But their presence also prevented Rodgers from reaching for any water. It was a warm day. No one tried to assassinate him. He won. But he was very thirsty.

Bill Rodgers at about mile 16 in 1980.

Did you know?

The average runner uses 2,600 calories to run a marathon but 500,000 in training for one.

The Finnish Connection

An inordinate number of Finnish runners have won or run well in the Boston Marathon. Such a record was not an accident. The Finnish-American community had a long-lasting and strong support for Finnish marathon runners.

Into the seventies, various Finnish-American organizations identified and sponsored top Finnish runners. The visiting Finnish runners were welcomed into the hospitable arms of the Finnish-American community for weeks before the race. This inspired many a young Finnish marathoner to train hard, and many excellent international marathon racing careers got their start by aiming for Boston.

Finnish runner Olavi Suomalainen in 1972.

Brookline Runner

RANIA MATAR came to Boston from her native Lebanon in 1987 to study architecture. Hearing of the Boston Marathon, she rose to its challenge in 1993. She wore a number provided by the B.A.A. to the Greater Boston Track Club in appreciation for all the help local running clubs give to the Marathon. Matar ran 3:45. Now she has a new challenge: twin girls, Lara and Samer. She trains while pushing them in a double baby jogger on the Marathon course in Brookline.

THEY WILL COME BACK

Five members of the Greater Boston Track Club left Boston to continue their careers on the West Coast. All had run in the Boston Marathon but moved to the Bay Area in recent years. California was a great place to continue running because of the ideal weather, and the running community was tight-knit, but when they heard of the Boston Marathon bombing in 2013, in a flash their hearts returned to Boston.

The members wanted to run the marathon again to show their defiance of the bombing, to show their community with Boston that had been their home for an important part of their younger running careers. They had moved on, or so they thought, until the bombings pulled them back. But they had no qualifying times.

To get their Boston qualifiers, they traveled north from their new Bay Area homes to Santa Rosa in wine country. Sloan Siegrist Palmore had taken her Harvard degree in microbiology to a job at Cal-Berkeley, had a baby, and raced to fifth woman in Santa Rosa with a time of 3:17:31. Christy Bonstelle, newly married and working in California, ran ninth in 3:21:17. Katie Famous, who got her medical degree at Boston University and now practices medicine in

The members wanted to run the marathon again to show their defiance of the bombing, to show their community with Boston that had been their home for an important part of their younger running careers.

San Francisco, ran 3:31:40 for 32nd place. Julie McGee, a physical therapist with a degree from the University of Massachusetts and a native of Needham, Massachusetts, ran 3:31:15. All had run faster in their Boston days and plan to do so again in Boston in 2014. It will be their homecoming.

Boston in BACK BAY

Boston is rich in Revolutionary American history. It is often considered symbolic of America and American freedom and democracy.

The Back Bay area is new land. In the 1800s, trains brought gravel from quarries in Needham to fill in the tidal flats at the mouth of the Charles River. The top of Beacon Hill was leveled off to help fill the Back Bay.

Modern Boston, with a population of 636,000 over some 90 square miles, holds every kind of neighborhood from posh to impoverished and every kind of ethnic group from pre-Revolutionary African Americans to recently arrived Cambodians. Thus the city is as diverse as the runners who come from all over the world to run the Marathon.

The Story of the Laurel Wreath

The laurel wreath is not a traditional prize for winning the Boston Marathon. The prize originally was a gold and diamond medal. Now the prize is money. But the laurel wreath is something different. It is a recognition of victory and symbolic of victory's limited durability. The leaves of the small European evergreen called *laurus nobilis* keep their color and shape for a long time. A crown fashioned from laurel leaves lasts, but not as long as a crown of gold. The victors are temporary royalty.

In the past, the most precious laurel for Boston Marathon winners came from trees in Greece. Greek-American George Demeter went through great difficulties to obtain fresh Greek laurel leaves in time for each Boston Marathon. At the finish line, he would chase the winner across the line and crown him as he crossed. During World War II, the Nazis owned the Greek laurels, so California laurel was used instead. Now laurel for the Boston Marathon wreaths comes from Greece courtesy of the Greek consulate in Boston.

Boston Runners

DOTTY FINE, a Boston resident for 23 years, runs now as a master. She lives a few blocks from the finish line in the Back Bay. She had taken up running for fitness in the seventies but the Marathon proved to be irresistible. "The last time I ran, I had a wonderful time running in a flying wedge for 18 miles with my Greater Boston Track Club teammates . . . we all finished well."

KAREN CROUNSE, 31 years old, has run the Boston Marathon seven times. She grew up in Wellesley, "very aware of the Marathon." She went to Wesleyan University, where Marathon winners Amby Burfoot and Bill Rodgers are alumni. When she moved to Brighton, she joined Bill Rodgers' old running club, the Greater Boston Track Club.

Attorney **PAMELA DUCKWORTH** lives a block off the Marathon course on Beacon Street. She has run the race 12 times. She also hosts runners from all over the world in her spacious house. Women's masters winner Evy Palm and her husband Uls of Sweden have stayed with her, as have runners from New Zealand, Colorado, Utah, and Alaska. She says, "I'll always participate in one way or another."

Did you know?

Massachusetts State Police estimate that 1½ to 2 million people watch the Boston Marathon in person. Media estimates maintain that another 120 million households are reached worldwide.

A Very Large Press Event Indeed

On Marathon weekend, 70 people work the B.A.A. press office. They issue 1,100 press badges to over 300 media outlets. Reporters from 100 U.S. newspapers come to cover the race, along with 30 television stations, 32 magazines, and 30 radio stations.

TV Tokyo sends a crew of 30. Crews also have come from Germany and Korea. Reporters have come from Israel, Australia, and South Africa.

In terms of on-site media coverage, the Boston Marathon ranks behind only the Super Bowl as the largest single-day sporting event in the world.

The press meet in the Copley Plaza Ballroom in 1995.

A scaffold of cameras recording the event.

Rosie Ruiz Pulls a Fast One

To those used to thinking of Boston as "proper" and full of "blue-bloods," Rosie Ruiz was just the ticket. She jumped into the race in Kenmore Square and ran only the last mile of the 1980 Boston Marathon, finishing before all the women. Officials immediately hoisted her up onto the awards platform, crowned her with laurels, and hung the gold medal around her neck. She played the astonished winner to the hilt, pulling off the ruse for the moment.

Rosie Ruiz.

Doubts quickly surfaced, however, and after a week of front-page newspaper headlines the B.A.A. disqualified her. As the wheels of history continued to grind, she turned out to be a pathological liar and a criminal rather than a merry prankster, but she went down in American folklore anyway. She never gave the medal back.

The Boston Red Sox

In 1916 the Boston Red Sox played what was billed as the first Marathon day game. They played the Washington Senators in a doubleheader, losing the first 3–2 and winning the next 2–0. Many games, however, had been previously and coincidentally held on Patriots Day.

The first Boston professional ballgame played opposite the Marathon was played by the Boston Americans, an early name for the Red Sox, on Saturday, April 19, 1902, against the Baltimore Orioles at the Huntington Avenue Grounds.

Through 2013, the Red Sox's record on Patriots Day is 68–50, and since 1959 every Red Sox Patriots Day game was scheduled at home to coincide with the running of the Marathon—except for an off day in 1967 and in 1995, when the baseball strike delayed the season.

Traditionally, baseball fans file out of Fenway Park and crowd Kenmore Square either elated because the Sox have won or depressed because they have lost. As soon as the first Marathon runner passes, the fans forget about baseball and become Marathon fans.

Fenway Park.

The Medical Tent

Curiously, those runners most in need of medical attention are not the fastest runners or the slowest but those who finish right around the prestigious three-hour mark. That's the finish time for most of the 600 or so runners who collapse. In the medical tent, about 10 percent of them receive intravenous feeding to replace quickly the three to four liters of water lost during the race.

The Boston Marathon pioneers in this type of treatment. Depending on how hot the day's weather, 5 to 15 percent of the entrants will need medical attention. Dehydration is the most serious problem, but blisters and other foot problems are the most common.

The medical tent at the finish line has 240 cots, while along the course 600 medical people wait to help any distressed runner. Twenty-five doctors, 75 nurses, and 100 podiatrists as well as athletic trainers and other medical specialists volunteer to help. This team has grown since 1978, when the medical staff was 12 volunteers.

In 1982 the medical team treated winner Alberto Salazar, who suffered from severe dehydration. Later, neurologist Roger Bannister—the first man to run a mile in under four minutes—noted that Salazar must have some ongoing medical problem. Subsequent tests showed that Salazar indeed had a condition that did not limit his sweat loss while running.

Runners receive state-of-the-art treatment in the medical tent.

The Finish Lines

The first three Marathons finished during a track meet on the Irvington Oval at the B.A.A. clubhouse. Then the finish was moved to just in front of the B.A.A. clubhouse on Exeter Street at the present location of the Boston Public Library. In 1965 the finish was moved to the west to Ring Road just off Boylston Street. In 1986 the finish moved east down Boylston Street to a location beside the Boston Public Library.

Spectators can watch on the Diamond screen, a huge video screen set up near the finish.

The Marathon course shrank between 1951 and 1956. No one could understand why times became suddenly much faster. Runners were astonished at their improvement. But their times in other races were not as good. Was this Boston magic? Nope. No one had noticed that various small improvements to the roads over many years had straightened them and shortened the course, although the starting and finishing lines had not been moved. Corrections were made after 1957, but the course was still off—probably 80 yards too long—until 1965, when it was corrected again. Of course, some runners feel the course was always "too long."

The old Exeter St. finish line.

Eliot Lounge

Until it closed in 1996, the Eliot Lounge was the runner's bar in Boston. On any night you could find someone who had something to do with running at the Eliot Lounge on Massachusetts Avenue. The walls were adorned with memorabilia, including photographs of all the Marathon greats. Tommy Leonard held court there.

Leonard, who has run in the Boston Marathon himself, was the head bartender and the official "greeter" of the Boston Marathon. Leonard may not have been the fastest marathoner in Boston history, but he's known and served the best. In fact, he is the best purveyor of greetings in the city. When you went into the Eliot Lounge, you got a warm hello with your cold one.

When Bill Rodgers dropped out of the 1977 Boston Marathon after losing his duel with eventual winner Jerome Drayton of Canada, he headed for the Eliot. As the rest of the racers ran by, Rodgers sought comfort there.

Tommy Leonard at the Eliot Lounge.

Hollywood in Boston

As in Hollywood, the stars of the Boston Marathon have donated their footprints to commemorate the race. Under the sidewalk superintendency of Boston mayor Tom Menino, four-time winner Bill Rodgers, official greeter Tommy Leonard, six-time-victorious coach Bill Squires, third-place finisher Bob Hodge, and many-time world cross-country champion Lynn Jennings, who ran Boston in 1978 when she was 17, pushed their feet into wet concrete in front of the Eliot Lounge on Massachusetts Avenue. The Eliot Lounge, city workers, and concrete mixers plan to continue the tradition.

From left, Bill Squires, Lynn Jennings, Geoff Smith, Bill Rodgers, Johnny Kelley, and Tommy Leonard leave their mark outside the Eliot Lounge in 1993.

Women Become Official At Last

Women ran the Boston Marathon for five years before B.A.A. officials agreed to issue numbers to them. Now tens of thousands of women run marathons, and it is hard to believe that as recently as 1971 there were only a handful. At first, B.A.A. officials lumped women in with those who regard the Marathon as a way to publicize their causes. But when women started to compete regularly and finish respectably, the B.A.A. realized that they were serious and wanted to race. Women were then welcomed.

The first official women's winner of the Boston Marathon was Nina Kuscsik from New York in 1972 . She won her race easily, 10 minutes ahead of the next woman to finish. Kuscsik later went on to hold important positions in the advocacy for women's long-distance running in the Olympics. It was another 12 years before there was a marathon for women in the Olympics.

Wanda Panfil, winner in 1991.

Hereford Street

Hereford Street is the short street that connects the long stretch down Commonwealth Avenue with the straight shot to the finish. It was on this little stretch in 1988 that Juma Ikangaa and Ibrahim Hussein ran shoulder to shoulder, neither yielding an inch, about to run to the closest finish in the race's history.

In 1971, Pat McMahon of the B.A.A. ran next to Alvaro Mejia of Colombia. On Hereford Street, the Colombian started his sprint, which deprived the B.A.A. of a second victory in its own Marathon.

In 1982, Dickie Beardsley and Alberto Salazar raced each other to Hereford Street, where Salazar gathered a little lead—he won by two seconds.

In 1978, Jeff Wells pursued Bill Rodgers and firmly believed, as he ran onto Hereford Street, that he would catch Rodgers and prevent his second victory, but such was not to be.

In 1987, Steve Jones and Geoff Smith, working together, chased Toshihiko Seko from the start. On Hereford Street, by mutual agreement, they dissolved their pact. Seko was too far ahead, and Smith and Jones sprinted against each other for second place.

The last good turn at Hereford Street.

The B.A.A.

A collection of Boston's wealthy and influential men with a profound and Christian interest in athletics met in the offices of Robert F. Clark in January of 1887. They met to draw up plans for a new athletic club. The membership fee would be $40 with annual dues of $30.

The B.A.A. shooting range.

In the early days, the Boston Athletic Association's track meet was a major event and the Marathon only an afterthought, finishing around the Irvington Street Oval. The B.A.A. conducted major sporting events in Boston and sponsored boxing matches and track meets. It had its own boathouse on the Charles River, its own shooting range, its own golf course and tennis courts. The elaborate B.A.A. clubhouse had a swimming pool.

A collection of Boston Athletic Association medals.

The B.A.A. fell on hard times during the Depression. They lost the clubhouse and other properties and moved first across the street to the Hotel Lenox and later to the Boston Arena. By the fifties, the organization—with only its Marathon and an indoor track meet left—had shrunk to a couple of events without any real assets. After the indoor track meet ceased, the B.A.A. existed only as an idea and some papers in a cardboard box on the floor of Jock Semple's trainer's room at the Boston Garden. Now the B.A.A. once again has full offices and staff.

The Military Relay

In 1918 the Great War raged, and the B.A.A. wanted to help the war effort. They decided to run the race as a 10-man military relay over the Marathon route. Each man, dressed in his service uniform, ran 2.5 miles carrying a baton.

As an athletic event, it did not work well. Men do not run fast in boots and long pants, although the army's drab contrasted well with the navy whites. The public paid little attention. The teams ran slowly and did not break the course record. One member of the relay team had run faster than his entire team when he placed 11th in 1911.

The army won.

The *Boston Herald* featured the army relay team in 1918.

B.A.A. Clubhouse

On May 1, 1887, ground was broken for the new B.A.A. clubhouse on Exeter Street opposite the Hotel Lenox. Completed in December of 1888, the clubhouse was a wonder of its day. Designed by architect J. H. Sturgis, it offered every amenity: bowling alleys, billiards, bicycling room, running track, tennis court, swimming pool, boxing room, fencing room, a barbershop, a restaurant, and a wine and cigar department.

The clubhouse had a Turkish bath with walls of glazed brick and horseshoe arches with decorations in Persian patterns, highlighted with medallions and circular stained glass windows. Every detail welcomed the man of wealth, worldliness, and power.

Many of those men lost their wealth during the Great Depression, and so did the B.A.A. The club could not pay its taxes or interest obligations. The B.A.A. clubhouse became Boston University's Soden Building until it was torn down to build the Boston Public Library annex.

The old B.A.A. clubhouse in 1914.

The Hotel Lenox

Perhaps the grandest guest at the Hotel Lenox was four-time Boston Marathon champion Gerard Cote. After his victories, he held court in his room for friends and reporters. There he smoked his victory cigar and drank the finest cognac available. For a short time, Cote—a man who trained up to 50 miles a day—lived lavishly.

The Lenox Hotel today.

During the war years, his celebrating got him in trouble with the Canadian army, in which he was a soldier. Although on leave and behaving reasonably, citizens complained when a photograph of Cote, obviously enjoying himself, feet up and cigar in hand in the luxury of the Lenox, appeared in newspapers while millions of Canadian soldiers awaited battle in Europe.

A floor of the Lenox served as B.A.A. headquarters in the late thirties. To this day the right room—the one on the corner of Exeter Street and Boylston—is a coveted place from which to watch the Marathon finish in comfort and luxury.

The Results

All but the elite runners at the head of the race are channeled through the chute system in which runners queue up to have their finishes recorded. The times are all processed by computer these days, and they are posted for all to see at the end of the day.

In the past, the winner received a crown of laurel and the gold medal. Cups or trophies went to the next seven finishers. The rest of those who crossed the line all got the same thing: a bowl of traditional beef stew.

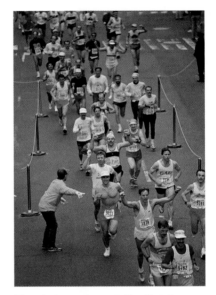

The chute system at the finish.

Did you know?

Beef Stew

(Recipe for 2,000 runners ca. 1970)

245 pounds potatoes	55 pounds peas
122 pounds onions	750 pounds beef chuck chunks
190 pounds carrots	108 gallons beef gravy

Place in large pot and cook for a long time.

(Courtesy Hugh Kinland, Stouffer's)

Marathon Winners

Male Winners

🇺🇸	1897	JOHN J. MCDERMOTT
🇨🇦	1898	RONALD J. MACDONALD
🇺🇸	1899	LAWRENCE J. BRIGNOLIA
🇨🇦	1900	JOHN P. CAFFERY
🇨🇦	1901	JOHN P. CAFFERY
🇺🇸	1902	SAMMY MELLOR
🇺🇸	1903	JOHN C. LORDEN
🇺🇸	1904	MICHAEL SPRING
🇺🇸	1905	FRED LORZ
🇺🇸	1906	TIMOTHY FORD
🇨🇦	1907	TOM LONGBOAT
🇺🇸	1908	THOMAS MORRISSEY
🇺🇸	1909	HENRI RENAUD
🇨🇦	1910	FRED CAMERON
🇺🇸	1911	CLARENCE H. DEMAR
🇺🇸	1912	MIKE RYAN
🇺🇸	1913	FRITZ CARLSON
🇨🇦	1914	JAMES DUFFY
🇨🇦	1915	EDOUARD FABRE
🇺🇸	1916	ARTHUR ROTH
🇺🇸	1917	BILL KENNEDY
🇺🇸	1918	CAMP DEVENS
🇺🇸	1919	CARL LINDER
🇬🇷	1920	PETER TRIVOULIDES
🇺🇸	1921	FRANK ZUNA
🇺🇸	1922	CLARENCE H. DEMAR

Male Winners

1923	CLARENCE H. DEMAR	
1924	CLARENCE H. DEMAR	
1925	CHARLES MELLOR	
1926	JOHN C. MILES	
1927	CLARENCE H. DEMAR	
1928	CLARENCE H. DEMAR	
1929	JOHN C. MILES	
1930	CLARENCE H. DEMAR	
1931	JAMES HENIGAN	
1932	PAUL DE BRUYN	
1933	LESLIE S. PAWSON	
1934	DAVE KOMONEN	
1935	JOHN A. KELLEY	
1936	ELLISON M. BROWN	
1937	WALTER YOUNG	
1938	LESLIE S. PAWSON	
1939	ELLISON M. BROWN	
1940	GERARD COTE	
1941	LESLIE S. PAWSON	
1942	BERNARD JOSEPH SMITH	
1943	GERARD COTE	
1944	GERARD COTE	
1945	JOHN A. KELLEY	
1946	STYLIANOS KYRIAKIDES	
1947	YUN BOK SUH	
1948	GERARD COTE	

Male Winners

Year	Winner	Year	Winner
1949	KARL GOSTA LEANDERSSON	1962	EINO OKSANEN
1950	KI-YONG HAM	1963	AURELE VANDENDRIESSCHE
1951	SHIGEKI TANAKA	1964	AURELE VANDENDRIESSCHE
1952	DOROTEO FLORES	1965	MORIO SHIGEMATSU
1953	KEIZO YAMADA	1966	KENJI KIMIHARA
1954	VEIKKO KARVONEN	1967	DAVID MCKENZIE
1955	HIDEO HAMAMURA	1968	AMBROSE BURFOOT
1956	ANTTI VISKARI	1969	YOSHIAKI UNETANI
1957	JOHN J. KELLEY	1970	RON HILL
1958	FRANJO MIHALIC	1971	ALVARO MEJIA
1959	EINO OKSANEN	1972	OLAVI SUOMALAINEN
1960	PAAVO KOTILA	1973	JON ANDERSON
1961	EINO OKSANEN	1974	NEIL CUSACK

Male Winners

1975	BILL RODGERS	1988	IBRAHIM HUSSEIN
1976	JACK FULTZ	1989	ABEBE MEKONNEN
1977	JEROME DRAYTON	1990	GELINDO BORDIN
1978	BILL RODGERS	1991	IBRAHIM HUSSEIN
1979	BILL RODGERS	1992	IBRAHIM HUSSEIN
1980	BILL RODGERS	1993	COSMAS NDETI
1981	TOSHIHIKO SEKO	1994	COSMAS NDETI
1982	ALBERTO SALAZAR	1995	COSMAS NDETI
1983	GREGORY A. MEYER	1996	MOSES TANUI
1984	GEOFF SMITH	1997	LAMECK AGUTA
1985	GEOFF SMITH	1998	MOSES TANUI
1986	ROB DE CASTELLA	1999	JOSEPH CHEBET
1987	TOSHIHIKO SEKO	2000	ELIJAH LAGAT

Male Winners

🇰🇷	2001	**LEE BONG-JU**
	2002	**RODGERS ROP**
	2003	**ROBERT KIPKOECH CHERUIYOT**
	2004	**TIMOTHY CHERIGAT**
	2005	**HAILU NEGUSSIE**
	2006	**ROBERT KIPKOECH CHERUIYOT**
	2007	**ROBERT KIPKOECH CHERUIYOT**
	2008	**ROBERT KIPKOECH CHERUIYOT**
	2009	**DERIBA MERGA**
	2010	**ROBERT KIPKOECH CHERUIYOT**
	2011	**GEOFFREY MUTAI**
	2012	**WESLEY KORIR**
	2013	**LELISA DESISA BENTI**

Female Winners

The flags represent the country for each winner for the women's race for each year, starting with Roberta Gibb's unofficial win in 1966. The first official winner was in 1972.

1966	ROBERTA GIBB	
1967	ROBERTA GIBB	
1968	ROBERTA GIBB	
1969	SARA MAE BERMAN	
1970	SARA MAE BERMAN	
1971	SARA MAE BERMAN	
1972	NINA KUSCSIK	
1973	JACQUELINE A. HANSEN	
1974	MICHIKO GORMAN	
1975	LIANE WINTER	
1976	KIM MERRITT	
1977	MICHIKO GORMAN	
1978	GAYLE BARRON	

1979	JOAN BENOIT	
1980	JACQUELINE GAREAU	
1981	ALLISON ROE	
1982	CHARLOTTE TESKE	
1983	JOAN BENOIT	
1984	LORRAINE MOLLER	
1985	LISA LARSEN WEIDENBACH	
1986	INGRID KRISTIANSEN	
1987	ROSA MOTA	
1988	ROSA MOTA	
1989	INGRID KRISTIANSEN	
1990	ROSA MOTA	
1991	WANDA PANFIL	

Female Winners

	1992	OLGA MARKOVA	2005	CATHERINE NDEREBA
	1993	OLGA MARKOVA	2006	RITA JEPTOO
	1994	UTA PIPPIG	2007	LIDIYA GRIGORYEVA
	1995	UTA PIPPIG	2008	DIRE TUNE
	1996	UTA PIPPIG	2009	SALINA KOSGEI
	1997	FATUMA ROBA	2010	TEYBA ERKESSO
	1998	FATUMA ROBA	2011	CAROLINE KILEL
	1999	FATUMA ROBA	2012	SHARON CHEROP
	2000	CATERINE NDEREBA	2013	RITA JEPTOO
	2001	CATERINE NDEREBA		
	2002	MARGARET OKAYO		
	2003	SVLETANA ZAKHAROVA		
	2004	CATHERINE NDEREBA		